THE SOUL OF
BUSINESS

THE SOUL OF
BUSINESS

Charles Garfield   Keshavan Nair
Lynne Twist   Willis Harman
David Whyte   Barry Schieber
Matthew Fox   Margaret Wheatley
Carol Orsborn   Myron Kellner-Rogers

with
Michael Toms

Hay House, Inc.
Carlsbad, CA

Published and distributed in the United States by:
Hay House, Inc., P.O. Box 5100, Carlsbad, CA 92018-5100
(800) 654-5126 • (800) 650-5115 (fax)

Edited by Michael Toms and the Hay House editorial staff
Editorial assistance: Rose Holland
Introduction, Prologues, and Epilogues by Michael Toms
Designed by Highpoint, Claremont, CA

Library of Congress Cataloging-in-Publication Data

The soul of business / Charles Garfield . . . [et al.] : with Michael Toms
        p. cm.
    ISBN 1-56170-377-X (pbk.)
     1. Social responsibility of business. 2. Management.
   3. Intellectuals--United States--interviews. I. Garfield, Charles A.
  II. Toms, Michael.
HD60.S667 1997
658.4'08--dc21   97-44786
                                             CIP

ISBN 1-56170-377-X

00 99 98 97   4 3 2 1
First Printing, December 1997

Printed in the United States of America

CONTENTS

PREFACE

About New Dimensions

New Dimensions Radio is the major activity of the New Dimensions Foundation, a nonprofit educational organization. "New Dimensions" is a national public radio interview series featuring thousands of hours of in-depth dialogues on a wide variety of topics. **Michael Toms,** the co-founder of New Dimensions Radio, and award-winning host of the "New Dimensions" radio interview series—and a widely respected New Paradigm spokesperson and scholar himself—engages in thoughtful, intimate dialogues with the leading thinkers and social innovators of our time focusing on positive approaches to the challenges of a changing society.

About This Book

A fundamental transformation is under way in the world of business and the workplace. This book is about this ongoing paradigm shift in the way business operates in the world. Moving beyond the traditional goals of productivity and profit, the new model of business for the 21st century embraces a more caring workplace: respect for the importance of spiritual values and vision, a commitment to empowering people to manifest their full creativity and passion, and recognizing the social responsibility of business to be a positive force for change in the world. Within the following pages, you will discover what promises to be a radical reorientation of the way business sees itself and functions in society, as well as how work and the workplace are changing.

Please Note: Throughout this book, the interviewer's questions are in italics.

✦ INTRODUCTION ✦

The purpose of this book is to demonstrate that a new ethic is emerging in the world of business, so readily perceived, often correctly, as greed-driven and self-concerned. This shift has to do with a realization that "the bottom line" is directly proportionate to the quality of the relationship between the organization and its employees, customers, suppliers, and all other corporate stakeholders. Put people first and profits will follow. A recent study of firms profiled in the *100 Best Companies to Work for in America* over an eight-year period revealed a 19.5 percent annual return for those companies during a period in which the 3,000 largest companies in the United States averaged a 12 percent annual return. It's true that the "old" ethic of the bottom-line mentality still dominates much of the corporate sector with downsizing, union busting, and reducing benefits very prevalent in the late 1990s.

However, the work of the contributors within this volume points to something different taking place in the business environment. Peak performance researcher **Charles Garfield** reveals the new story emerging in American business, one that sees the organization as a living system. Garfield is joined by fund-raiser extraordinaire **Lynne Twist** in the second chapter to focus on creating meaning and purpose through work as service. Poet **David Whyte** tells us about the importance of soul in the workplace. Author and business visionary **Carol Orsborn** shows the way to integrity in business. Management consultant **Keshavan Nair** applies the principles of Gandhi as the means to manifest soulful work. The late scientist and futurist **Willis Harman** points to a new business paradigm for the 21st century. Former investment advisor **Barry Schieber** relates the relevance of spiritual principles to work and business. **Margaret Wheatley** and **Myron Kellner-Rogers** bring their organizational development expertise to bear on how play and spontaneous action can create effective organizations.

This book provides a bridge to a new and exciting world of business, where people are of paramount importance and the bottom line reflects a commitment to the common good in all ways.

— Michael Toms
Ukiah, California
October 1997

✦ CHAPTER ONE ✦

The New Story in Business

Charles Garfield and Michael Toms

PROLOGUE

*M*ost *of us are aware that major changes are occurring in how we view the world around us. This shift from a mechanistic and linear view to a more organic and holistic perspective is permeating many professions and institutions. What many of us don't know is how this transformation is profoundly influencing the structure and function of the modern corporation. The new corporate organization is fluid, flexible, and adaptable, able to cope with chaos and operating interdependently with its environment.*

My interviewee, Dr. Charles Garfield, has been studying high achievers for a quarter century. He was a computer scientist on the Apollo 11 project that sent the first men to the moon. He later when on to found The Shanti Project, a nonprofit organization that provides support to patients and families facing life-threatening illnesses. He is a clinical professor at the University of California Medical School in San Francisco, and the author of the best-sellers, Peak Performers *and* Second to None: How Our Smartest Companies Put People First.

MICHAEL TOMS: *Charlie, one of the things you wrote about in* Second to None *is the new story of business. So tell us about the new story.*

CHARLES GARFIELD: The new story is a profoundly human-based story that moves us away from what I call "mechanocentric," machine-centered imagery and mythology, to an eco-systemic perspective, a living systems perspective. Imagine if instead of seeing our institutions, particularly corporate institutions and governmental institutions, as lean machines, we saw them as living systems that really understood what it takes to nourish the best in human beings, to nourish human beings at the highest levels of their potential.

So we are moving away from the idea that we have to get lean and mean in a tough economy?

All of that imagery is the imagery of an old story. It's the imagery of the lone pioneer, the rugged individualist—Horatio Alger. The person who theoretically was able to pull himself or herself up by the bootstraps alone and make it work. All in a jungle out there. What we are seeing now is that, that imagery, that mythology, that way of viewing the world, that paradigm, simply doesn't work anymore. We are living on an interdependent planet, and corporate systems are always subsystems of that interdependence, and they require collaboration and partnership. We're moving toward a fundamentally different understanding of what it takes to nourish human beings and to nourish living systems, called corporations or any other institution.

Do you see this kind of change occurring in leadership throughout the world, or just in America?

You certainly see it around the world, but you see it differently in different places. Nobody who knows business is going to say that this has emerged as the dominant paradigm. What we're saying is, we have moved past the time of parenthesis. Many of us, about ten years ago, were talking about being trapped between mythologies, between worldviews. I think we've moved out of that parenthesis. I think we're in the very beginning stages of the blossoming of the new story, a new mythology, the form of which is now becoming evident. We can see it, perhaps, through a mist and through veils, but we see some form taking shape. Even in the midst of what looks like a profoundly old story, which you certainly can see around the world, there are also strong examples of leadership of a new story emerging.

Anybody can point out a hundred old-story corporations that are operating mechanocentrically, as machines, not caring about human beings, seeing people as machine parts, as disposable work units, as widgets. You can also see, as we talked about in *Second to None*, very successful enterprises putting people first—in the sense of asking the question: What does it take to make this living system called a corporation, work best? What sort of values, what sort of structures, what do we need for the people working in these organizations so that they are most nourished and, hence, the corporation is most nourished? We're seeing people ask these questions in very intelligent ways now that we didn't see ten years ago.

Could we say that the emergence of democracies around the world is really a reflection of the death of the old leadership model?

Absolutely. What we see in Eastern Europe and what we saw in the fall of the Berlin Wall and the change in the former Soviet Union is what we are seeing within American corporations, albeit with less tumult and less chaos. We are seeing some of the very same forces at work. When we talk about decentralization, we're also talking about partnership, and we're talking about grass-roots empowerment. And, many of the other images and ideology that we're hearing now that came out of major changes in Eastern Europe, we're seeing also within the corporation. Did you ever notice how American corporate leaders will fight for democracy anywhere in the world except within their own companies? In their own companies, democracy is called socialism—giving too much power to the grass roots. We support democratic ideals everywhere else except here in our companies. The old story is experiencing its early death throes, its sunset effect. We're hearing many very intelligent corporate leaders say that these forces have been unleashed.

I'm thinking of Lee Iacocca, who was profiled in Peak Performers *as someone who would jump from one corporation to another and transform the company, and more recently had basically decided that he was different and above the worker at Chrysler.*

It really is different. In *Peak Performers,* what we said was, here was somebody that came along and was able to handle crisis, was able to handle chaos. That always was his strong suit. He never appeared to be a great manager who could deal with complex processes over the long haul. He's a Winston Churchill kind of character—in terms of style—who's able to come in and take charge when things are tough. That's exactly what the individualist lone-pioneer style was about. When things got more process oriented, when success required strategic alliances around the world or within the country, when it required really linking up as partners with your workers at the front line, old-story corporate leaders struggled and stumbled. They understand some things extraordinarily well, but they tended to worship the numbers rather than understanding human beings and human process.

Is this new leadership model really changing the profile and the look of the Peak Performer?

It's changing the Peak Performer from the lone pioneer, the rugged individualist, to the fully participating partner. It's the person who knows how to collaborate well, partner well with other human beings, be a team player, who now emerges as the peak performer of the '90s and beyond.

The former Peak Performer in some ways was peak-performing in spite of the corporate environment, and now there's a more co-operative Peak Performer emerging.

That's exactly right. At one point in 1986, after the Challenger disaster, I really took a close look at what happened there and how different it was from the Apollo 11 mission I worked on. I realized that there was something perverse about a model of achievement that required us to thrive in spite of our own organizations. Many people who are high achievers, when they think of their own work situations, probably would admit that they thrive despite the company, despite the team they work in. What if we had another model—companies that thrived because their people thrived. A congruence between organizational well-being and individual well-being. That's what's staring to emerge now.

One of the things you touched on was the emergence of democracy within the corporation. How is that happening?

What we're seeing now is a move toward more collaborative decision making, a trusting of the front line, of people at the very modest levels of organizational life, and an understanding that all the technical decision making, sales and marketing decision making, and other essentials of the company has to include those who actually do the hands-on work. They are no longer just hired hands. The great wisdom of organizations includes the wisdom possessed by the people who are out in the world with customers called salespeople, and unless they give voice to their vision and we allow that voice to be heard, we're going to lose tremendously important information. We stay isolated in the executive suite or boardroom where we make decisions based upon our own view of things, not based upon the day-to-day realities of our customers or workforce. And so the wise corporate leaders right now understand democracy in terms of allowing decision making to happen in a very collaborative way. Information is to be shared, there is generous sharing of profit and reward, and a generous sharing of technology and utilization of technology. These kinds of things are happening in a much more democratic way than ever before, even though the word *democracy* isn't used much in day-to-day corporate life.

Now again, we are at the beginning stages of this. It looks very much like the ideals that we would call democratic. And you might ask, Why are these changes happening? Are these idealists who realize that this is best for human beings? I wish I could say that. If you were to pin me down to one reason for the emergence of what appears to be a democratic-like context, I would say that it works, it's functional. It works better than the models we've been using.

It works better, certainly, in the midst of great change.

It works better in the midst of great change, and it works from the point of view of human beings as well as the organization itself.

This would be compared to the usual, the old form of the hierarchical and almost dictatorial kind of company?

That simply doesn't work in a fast-paced environment. By the time you send the memo up the chimney and get 12 approvals, and by the time it comes down to you, it may be so far removed from the original impulse that led to the request that you don't care anymore, and besides, three of your competitors have acted on this issue six months ago. In the old model, in the old hierarchical story of business, people were so afraid of taking any action because only two things could happen. If they succeeded, somebody else would take credit for it, and if they failed, their neck was on the line. So what did they learn? They learned to take no risks, do exactly what you know how to do and what you are authorized to do. And if you see something very dangerous happening, don't say anything because you could be wrong and be labeled a naysayer. You could be right and be put in charge of it. You couldn't possibly win.

You did uncover some people who were able to be innovative and creative in the midst of that kind of environment. I think of Chuck House of Hewlett-Packard.

It was an interesting interview. We wrote about it in *Peak Performers*. We covered him a lot more extensively in *Second to None*. Hewlett-Packard gets a lot of attention, I think rightfully so for being innovative and progressive in many ways. It also has its share of tradition-bound individuals, a board of directors that one would describe as old-story folks. That's where they learned their lessons, and those are the lessons they hold dear. Here's a man whose capacity for innovation is considerable and would love to be able to move more rapidly and has managed to harness what I call a covert culture.

Every organization has an overt culture (rules and regulations and policies), and a covert culture (the way things really work around here, how do you really get it done—how do you tap the resources that the company itself doesn't know it has?). Well, Chuck

House is a very, very talented man at utilizing the forces that operate in the covert culture. He can get things done despite the stultifying effects of large organizations. He is fascinating as a result of that. Many of the inspirations in *Second to None* were people like Chuck House, in companies large and small around this country, who were able to achieve a great deal despite the fact that the overarching culture (organizational culture) was fairly stultifying.

He was actually told by David Packard himself not to work on a large video screen that would be high resolution, and he just went ahead and worked on it anyway.

Yes, and imagine the courage. He succeeded. The company was wise enough to celebrate his achievement and gave him this award for contempt and noncompliance because he had the courage not to back off when the leader told him to. I guess the interesting message to this story is how much innovative capacity and creativity is clipped and eradicated because organizations have no tolerance for the very people who could save them.

It also brings to mind one of the things that's been happening, particularly in the American economy, with companies downsizing and getting rid of people. And there are companies that are just getting rid of people carte blanche—just chop, chop, chop. And then there are companies that are paying a little more attention to that process. What about that?

It's a perfect example of the difference between an organization as a machine and an organization as an ecosystem. As a machine, if you need to make a more efficient machine, one way is to get rid of what you perceive to be unnecessary parts. Lean and mean, disposable parts, disposable work units, get rid of all sorts of people because, of course, salaries are our greatest expense. That's what the machine paradigm would say. The ecosystem would say, What about the survivors? What about all those people who are watching? My buddy George has been here for 30 years. He got great evaluations each time. He was very valued. He had a lot of knowledge. He was the one who took care of us throughout many of our problems, and he was let go. In fact, he came in one day, and the lock on his door was changed and his name plaque was off, and his desk was in the corridor. No one even said anything to him.

I would only ask people who believe in the machine story to consider that the survivors are watching. They will never trust you again once they see that, such as downsizing. The ecosystem story understands that you have to tap the wisdom of this ecosystem called a company. And say simply, Here's what we face. This is what we need to save, this dollar amount, for instance. What creative ideas can we generate in order to save this amount? People will come up with job sharing. They will do some things that were outsourced. They'll come up with many creative ideas for saving the company the amount of money that would perhaps be saved in the kind of needlessly painful downsizing.

We see wonderful companies in *Second to None*. Semco in Brazil did marvelous kinds of things with regard to their company in order to get it in running shape without really eliminating human beings. They tapped the upper levels of the capabilities of the people on board. They turned the decisions of what to do over to the group that had to do it—namely, the employees of the company.

One of the examples you cited in Second to None *was Levi Strauss and their downsizing and what they did with the employees they let go.*

A company like that has had a long history of really understanding human beings. They decided to turn over much of the decision making to employees to retrain them and to provide them with health support—because this is a terribly stressful period—to help them find jobs, to give them generous financial considerations upon leaving. Even then they would say that they probably didn't communicate well enough, even though they communicated a great deal. What I said to the people I interviewed for the book was, You're not dealing with people who are in normal frames of mind. These are people who've been shocked. Anybody who knows anything about a shock reaction knows that even if you say it to them two or three or four times, they may not hear you, so you may need to communicate over and over again. They were a very impressive example. Compare them with some of the other companies, people you read about, and companies you read about in the paper all the time. Closing factories here and there, just simply giving notice. Thirty days. It's over. Minimal consideration for the people who've been there for decades.

What about the example you cited about Wells Fargo's acquisition of Crocker?

Yes, and another would be Safeway's situation in their leveraged buy-out with KKR in the mid-'80s. What you're seeing are organizations that are certainly pressured by market forces and outside factors, but which are choosing a strategy that makes it terribly difficult for the human beings of their companies. How can either of those companies face any of those people who went through that period and say that this company sees people as a very valuable resource. We're a big happy family. In other words, to say all the things you have to say to have a collaborative effort work. How can they ever say that again? People who lived through it don't feel like the greatest resource.

In the case of Wells Fargo, they went on to greater profits and to be the most profitable bank in California? What about that?

Short-term, you can make great gains by documenting that hundreds or thousands of salaries have been axed. Now your bottom line looks much better in the shorter term. My question is: What happens to the health of the corporate organism long-term? Take a look at them later—many of these companies are struggling. If you go into a store—and I don't want to pick on one company—but if you go into a store, just watch the people doing the work. Look in their eyes, watch how they respond to customers. I'm fond of asking people questions when I'm in checkout lines: How's it going around here? Do you like this place? That's all you have to say. You'll get all you want.

Justine [Michael Toms's wife] and I live in a rural area. But there is a Safeway. And one of the things that's consistent whenever we happen to shop there, whenever you go through the checkout line, is that the checkers are always talking about when the next break is. It is absolutely consistent. It never fails.

It may stun you to realize that it's not even rural versus urban. It's the culture in many organizations. You find people who look depressed, look upset, and can't wait for the next break. Now anybody in that situation would be feeling much the same thing.

What happens in these downsized situations where people are axed is that the remaining employees wind up getting double and triple workloads.

That's exactly what happens. They end up having to do two jobs, to wear multiple hats and to be responsible for all sorts of things that they may not have been trained for particularly well. They have to do that in the midst of a downsizing—in other words, firing of many of their friends, which teaches them a very, very important rule: This place can be dangerous. It could be me next. In fact, it could have been me last time but for the grace of God.

Employees are asked to do a lot more at a time in which their suspicions are highest, their trust is lowest. It's like a dysfunctional family, except you've got multiple parents and siblings all over the place, and you don't know whom to trust or what to do.

You've talked about a company in Brazil that is interesting because the chief executive actually takes 45 to 60 days off a year and travels and never lets anyone know where he is. Tell us about that.

Ricardo Semler, the chief executive of Semco and its owner, takes even more than 45 to 60 days. He goes away for months at a time, and people can't contact him. It was awfully hard for us to set up the interview with him. He does it for a number of reasons. He's at a point in his life where he has the resources, and he wants to live a life that he finds maximally fulfilling. There's another reason, which I think is frankly brilliant. He wants to let everybody know that the lone pioneer model, the big boss in the big office at the top of the pyramid, is a model that simply doesn't work. He wants everybody else in the company to know that he's not as indispensable as everybody thinks their boss is. He wants people to trust their own resources. He wants them to deal with the day-to-day problems without him and to prove to themselves and the organization that they can do a mighty fine job. And it's working. It's working very well.

This executive has taken some rather fascinating trips. Tell us about some of them.

On one trip he duplicated Marco Polo's original journey, on another he trekked through the Himalayas, and on another trip he went to the North Pole. He does the kinds of things that I suspect many of us would want to do if we had the time, courage, and resources. I think the message to his company is: You will do just fine without me.

Another example with economic considerations being the cat-alytic agent was the example of ARCO. When the oil crisis occurred, ARCO, which had been a fairly progressive company, suddenly reverted back to the old model. Tell us about that.

ARCO had leadership that was really committed to the kinds of transformations I'm talking about—the human-centered systems, the living systems—and they were doing very well. Then they got hit by the oil crisis, the oil shortages of the '70s, and they got hit by economic factors that hit everybody, and that's the time in which the people with the black hats come out. Their basic message is: Get rid of all this touchy-feely stuff, anything having to do with human beings—never mind anything that's progressive from a human potential point of view.

Anything that has to do with human functioning is seen as touchy-feely stuff. Get rid of all that, and get tough. Now get tough means you can do anything you want as long as you say it's a business decision. It's for the good of the company. And unfortunately, they did a great deal of that. Short term? They were able to show that the bottom line prospered. A few years down field, they were in the same bind that all the other oil companies were. Little trust—many of their own people were afraid to trust them. And now they've cycled back out of that and have established themselves—at least within the category of oil companies—as one of the more progressive ones. Still, they don't have the visionary leadership that they had earlier when they really had the promise of being one of the really interesting new-story companies.

You also interviewed some sports coaches. Tell us about that.

I've had a long-term interest in not only the space program and my involvement there, but in the sports world. I wanted to take a look at leadership at the highest level of sport. So I picked the most successful professional coaches in the three major sports.

Tony LaRussa, formerly of the Oakland As and now the St. Louis Cardinals; Bill Walsh, when he was coach of the San Francisco 49ers; and Pat Riley, who was coach of the Los Angeles Lakers, the New York Knicks, and now the Miami Heat. What was interesting was that in all three cases, they knew about a book I wrote called *Peak Performance* on mental-training techniques for athletes. They knew about the principles in the book, and so they were already predisposed toward harnessing the power, the potential of human beings—not only on a purely physical/mechanical level, but on a mental-emotional level.

In all three cases, they taught me more than I knew about teamwork and what the nature of teamwork is when results are very intensely monitored and very visible to all who care to look. In all three cases, they understood human beings extremely well. I wouldn't say that any of them were always masters one-to-one, although they worked well one-to-one with some people. They understood how the organism called a team actually functioned as a living system. They had better or worse relationships with individual players. Pat Riley probably has the best one-to-one relationship sense of all of them. All three of them had that sense of a team as a living organism, and I really learned a lot from them.

Bill Walsh is known as a cold turkey kind of coach. During Walsh's era, there were frequently players who had reached a certain plateau in his eyes, and he would just chop 'em and they were gone.

That was a different situation, then. There was less of a long-term process sense than with a corporation. Their results are monitored weekly, and major decisions about their futures, athletes and coaches, made yearly. This is not quite the same as a corporate organization or government organization. Walsh was able to see when a certain element in that eco-system called a professional football team had reached its maximum utility. He saw it earlier than almost everybody else. The fact that players are let go—there's no doubt that that's the way the professional game is played.

You pretty much have a choice. You can play out allegiances to people longer than their functional capabilities will allow, in which case you'll have a group that really loves you, but you'll finish last. Or you develop some way of developing collaborative understanding that elements of this ecosystem have to be replaced, as in any other ecosystem, and do it as humanely as possible. I don't think that Bill Walsh's interpersonal sense was the part of himself that he values the most. He's a very functional leader, but he's in a very functional context. I won't call him a new-story leader in the sense of understanding long-term processes, but that's not the arena that he's chosen.

It is interesting that after he departed, the 49ers had their most controversial exit of three of their most popular players: Joe Montana, Ronnie Lott, and Roger Craig. I don't think that would have happened quite that way if Bill Walsh had been there.

No, I don't think it would have happened. He would have figured out another way to do it or another timing for it. There is an elegance about the man in the sense that even when the decisions he makes are controversial, the logic and the intelligence of those decisions tend not to be questioned because people assume that he knows what he's doing and, in fact, in most cases he does. Those were very interesting interviews with the coaches. I wanted to take a look at one of the primary arenas for achievement in this culture and to take a look at what transformative elements, what mythic elements, were emerging in sport as well as in business. I'm not making a strong case for major transformation there because it's not as evident as it is where longer processes, like in a corporation, exist.

Relating this to practical concerns such as the environment in this country, we have examples of many corporations who continue to pollute, continue to destroy the environment. How long is it going to take for this corporate shift to happen?

Things change for a number of reasons. They change in an evolutionary sense slowly over time, in which case the humans who are living in the time of change are always disgruntled because it's not going fast enough. The planet has its own logic and its own time frame. The other model that has chaos theory at the heart of its operation is called "catastrophe." In other words, something very catastrophic happens. Now it may not be catastrophic from the planet's point of view. It certainly may be catastrophic from the human being's point of view, which shifts us into a new equilibrium. It shifts us out of our steady state into a new equilibrium. Things come together much differently after a time of chaos and disequilibrium.

Do you mean something like the ozone-layer depletion?

Sure. For years we feared the catastrophe was going to be a nuclear holocaust. Now it's some environmental problem like ozone depletion. But there's another kind of change, and I'm still in a frame of mind whereby this other one is very real to me, and I think it is for many others. Not only catastrophe, but benestrophe. Something very wonderful happening. Didn't that happen in Eastern Europe, at least in part? Now, they are struggling, yes. But wouldn't some of them say that something very wonderful happened almost magically as a result of years of tension and pressure? Could that happen in this country? Could that happen around the world? Some grass-roots movement that says that it must be different. The old way doesn't work. There must be a change. I still think, and I have reason to believe, since the writing of *Second to None,* that there are people increasing in numbers, gaining in power, gaining in influence, who could in fact be the precipitating element in a benestrophe, in massive good news, changing our worldview and our paradigm, changing to the new story.

I've never heard that word. It's a great word. Benestrophe?

Benestrophe. We don't even have a word for massive good news. We have a word for massive bad news, and everybody knows what it is. But *benestrophe.* Can we even conceive that something powerful, wonderful, and quick could happen? I think so.

We certainly didn't conceive it in the case of Eastern Europe and the Soviet Union. No one predicted that.

No one did, and so forces outside human awareness were operating that resulted in something that at least many of us hope is a powerful long-term force for good. I think that was in many ways benestrophic in its impact. Could that happen from an environmental point of view? Could we wake up? Could there be a wake-up call that we pay attention to, and could that wake-up call be a very positive wake-up call?

I'll give you one example. I visit with of a group of people from time to time in Nashville, Tennessee. It's a group called Kidsface. It's a group of kids concerned with the environment. Most people think, *Isn't that cute, they're concerned with the environment.* Well, all of a sudden in about two years' time, this little group that started in Nashville has chapters in all 50 states, chapters in 11 countries. The little girl who runs it, Melissa Poe, got invited to the big Rio conference as a speaker; she carried the Olympic torch. All of a sudden there's this movement of children. At first glance, it looks cute and not very powerful. I would submit to you that if the faces of children became a dominant image for us, and we were asked to confront the implications of our short-term action and had to face those children and look at those faces, look at those images, then the psychological impact of that sustained look would be enough to move many people toward grass-roots action.

I would love to take some of the chief executives of those companies that are feigning ecological commitment and ask them to look into the eyes of their children and grandchildren, especially the littlest ones, and say to them, I'm really sorry, but I'm going to pollute your planet and jeopardize your life for the duration. Of course they wouldn't do that. So they have to deny to themselves that they are ever doing anything bad at all. Well, they need to be confronted with that in a way that's collaborative but strong, and I would love to see what would happen if we really admitted what we are doing to the next generation and the one after that. I would love to see the impact. I suspect that something would shift for many—not all, but many people. A shift that would have bene-strophic implications.

In going through the '80s and into the '90s, we've seen the example of, in some ways, the diminishing or inhibition or elimination of a lot of rules and regulations that used to protect people. I think of one example being the Occupational Safety and Health Administration, which is pretty well gutted as a federal agency, eliminated totally in the state of California. This was an agency that concerned itself with industrial accidents and industrial safety and that kind of thing. We have this old mythic idea that the fox is in charge of the henhouse. So we've come to this period where greed has been a dominant factor. Greed took precedence over any other considerations, particularly human considerations or future-generations considerations. What I'm getting at is the relationship of business and greed and profit to the political system and the structure itself. In some ways, these things couldn't have happened without those two things being hand-in-glove.

They are hand-in-glove, and the way they have been run, certainly in recent times, has been hand-in-glove. You could very easily see it in a statistic we hear a great deal: "One percent of the people have 85 percent of the money." Or "one percent of the people have 90 percent of the power." Whatever the specific percentages are, it's very clear that very, very few people wield power in a nondemocratic form, given what the founding fathers had in mind.

One has to see an intelligence behind what happened in the '80s through recent times. There may not have been values that were nourishing and healthy to the larger body politic and planet, but certainly there was an intelligence. I think what we've found now is that although that kind of narrow-minded intelligence is still very much with us, there have been the beginnings of an outcry. And the cry is: Never again! No more. Were we to allow the old story values to govern our conduct, we could very well die of it.

The problem with polluting a planet you're standing on is that eventually you die, too—as do all those you love. The problem with greed—in other words, nourishing one part of an ecosystem at the expense of all other parts, is that the whole ecosystem dies. The short-sightedness of the '80s and '90s greed was simply the lack of a systemic view. You don't go into a forest and take care of only one element in an ecosystem. You give it all the water, you give it all the nourishment, you give it all the nutrients it needs. We've been saying by our actions to all the other elements in the ecosystem, "You're getting nothing. It's a jungle out here. If only you were tough enough or bright enough, you would be among the one percent. Sorry, you get nothing."

What happens is, because of the interdependent rules of an ecosystem, the whole system suffers or dies. The same thing happens with economies and planets. I think that realization is emerging from the collective unconscious of the species to our conscious awareness. I think we are getting more and more offended, angry, irritated, and motivated to change that kind of short-sightedness.

I was thinking of your use of the term ecosystem *as related to corporations, and I'm thinking of the irony in the old-model bumper sticker that says: "Trees are a renewable resource." The environmentalists' battle to preserve some of the old-growth forests with protecting the spotted owl, and how the spotted owl is isolated as this single creature. It's sort of like spotted owl versus trees versus jobs, et cetera. That we're going to save this one bird, and we're going to give up jobs. It's missing the fact that the spotted owl is representative of an entire ecosystem, and you can never replace an old-growth forest unless you wait a thousand years. Trees are not a renewable resource in the sense that the old-growth forest is not renewable, except if you wait a thousand years.*

The ecosystem has its own logic. Systems have their own logic, and if you isolate one element of the system—that very strategy is indicative of an old-story, nonsystemic mentality, an old-story way of thinking. I think we need to consider more the deep ecological ethic. One that understands living systems. One that understands spirit. One that understands aliveness. One that especially understands the interconnectedness of all beings. Unless we learn to see in systemic ways, we will continue to isolate this organism and pit it against that organism and try to give more priority to one than the other. That's really missing the point. It's all of a piece, and if my end of the boat sinks, so does yours.

I think that many people have direct experience of the connection between how a corporation is run and the service one receives from that same corporation. Can you tell your story of flying on an airline that doesn't exist anymore, and perhaps one of the reasons it doesn't exist?

I'm a storyteller, and I'm a collector of stories from daily life, and I fly a lot. I fly to give speeches mostly. I only count on a couple of things when I fly. I count on a seat, which I don't always get because I can be bumped. That is, the airlines have seemingly rewritten capitalism. They can take my check, cash my check, put my money in their bank account, and send me a ticket. Now a ticket to the ball game means you get in the ball game. A ticket to the concert means you get in a concert. A ticket to the airline means you might get on the plane, but you might not get on the plane. Now that whole thing is terribly disconcerting if you have to be on stage to speak at nine the next morning.

Now the other thing I count on is a meal. I don't count on a very good meal, but something to keep the physiology alive, and I never forgot the time when the flight attendant came over and, instead of offering me one of two entrees that were available, simply said, "We've run out of both entrees. Would you take a dinner salad and coffee?" No food, and a long cross-country flight. The guy next to me was furious, so I couldn't get any work done. He got the same shabby treatment.

In order to get away from his badgering of the flight attendants over their lack of food, I decided to walk away and just stretch my legs and apologize to the flight attendants for my seatmate's shabby behavior. He was kind of rough with them. I went to the front of the plane where they were sitting, and there was this kitchen up there with a curtain over it, and I pulled the curtain aside, and the flight attendants were sitting there eating our entrees. They were eating our food. The food that was slotted for passengers was being eaten by the flight attendants. I had this shocked look on my face, so the flight attendant looked up and said, "Well, we've got to eat, too." I didn't know what to say, so I looked at my extremely irate seatmate, and said, "Ralph, come here." I had no words for it. It's as if, person-to-person diligence, service, had totally been suspended. That it didn't matter anymore. As if the service elements of the business were totally irrelevant. We had a certain amount of food, and it was dog-eat-dog, and whoever gets the food wins.

I think too many of us have had experiences on the downside—experiences in service contexts that simply didn't work.

Corporations are entities formed by people, run by people, and peopled by human beings very similar to the rest of us. Corporations can be very intense places exposing the worst, and occasionally the best, in human nature. I think what we are finding is not only promising, but gaining momentum. The new story of business is emerging during one of the most challenging times in business history. A transformation is occurring that is more profound than the changes in technology, globalization, management employee contract, and so on.

EPILOGUE

It is clear that there is, indeed, a new story emerging that redefines the nature of business and the corporate sector. We are entering a new era where creativity and compassion can flourish, and business is practiced as if people matter. The previously "faceless" corporate sector is beginning to show its human side, because the fact is that people are the lifeblood of any organization, and they are hungry for meaning and purpose and motivated by their innermost values. The future begins today, as each of us takes responsibility for making the workplace around us more caring and people oriented.

✦ Chapter Two ✦

The Spirit of Service

Lynne Twist, Charles Garfield, and Michael Toms

PROLOGUE

*L*ynne Twist and Charles Garfield speak to the transformative *spirit of service. To serve means trusting the deeper movement of spirit in our lives. In the process of opening our hearts and minds, we discover an inseparable connection between ourselves and the world. Service expresses this connection, quickening the transformation of both character and community. For some, service means helping a family member or neighbor. For others, it means volunteer work for the homeless, homebound people, people with AIDS, or children at risk. For many of us, it means choosing work imbued with the spirit of service, work that contributes to the healing of the world. Whatever our calling, each of us can contribute to creatively renewing our lives, our organizations, our communities, and our cultures through service.*

Our interviewees, Lynne Twist and Charles Garfield, are two *people whose lives and work are exemplary of service. Lynne Twist is one of the founding executives of The Hunger Project, an international not-for-profit organization dedicated to ending chronic, persistent hunger worldwide. Her leadership of The Hunger Project has been an important factor in the project's growth and development. She's been responsible for raising over $100 million, and has provided training and fund-raising technologies to Hunger Project volunteers and staff in more than 37 countries on five continents.*

Charles Garfield helped design the Apollo 11 Project, the first lunar landing module. And then he went on to found Shanti Project, recognized as a national model for programs working with people facing life-threatening illness. He has a number of books, including Peak Performers, Second to None, *and* Sometimes My Heart Goes Numb: Love and Caregiving in a Time of AIDS. *He's also a clinical professor of psychology at the University of California, San Francisco School of Medicine.*

MICHAEL TOMS: *Lynne, let's begin with how you got started doing your work.*

LYNNE: I was in the right place at the right time. I feel very guided to be doing what I'm doing. In the mid '70s in San Francisco, there was a lot of global thinking going on here, and maybe in other places in the world, although I certainly wasn't aware of it. And even the word *global* was kind of a strange word. Most people called everything international if it was outside the United States. There was a series of meetings that involved a great many impressive people, including Buckminster Fuller, Werner Erhard, John Denver, Dr. Robert Fuller, and others who were looking at major questions about humanity as we approached the last 25 years of the century and, in fact, the millennium. And one of the questions they asked (I think it was Bucky's question), was: What is the fundamental breakdown in human integrity, that if resolved, would produce a profound breakthrough for life? And it became clear to Bucky and to Werner and to some of the other people that millions and millions and millions of people were dying of hunger in a world that was awash with food. This was a breakdown—not in distribution or production—but a breakdown in human integrity, that we would allow that to continue.

I was fortunate enough to be witness to in some of those discussions, and out of them the Hunger Project was born, and I was fortunate enough to be around to be part of its early days. So I think I was just in the right place at the right time, and I was very eager to find a way to involve myself in making a significant difference in the quality of life. So it was a fit.

Something about the work must have been fulfilling to you, because you've stayed with it as long as you have.

LYNNE: I would say that it was really like an epiphany for me. I saw clearly that hunger was not something that we needed to somehow find a way to settle for, or allow to continue. It was such a mammoth problem. I actually saw for myself, with my own being, that it could be eradicated in my lifetime. It's sort of unthinkable, even now, but at *that* time it was really unthinkable. I didn't have a lot of facts, but I had the sense that this was something worth giving one's life to. And I did, almost in the first moment. And I have ever since. To me, it was a life-altering moment, and it has been a life-altering commitment.

Charlie, how about your involvement? How did that start for you?

CHARLES: I have the same sense that Lynne does. It chose me. I won't say right place at the right time, although in a sense that was true. I am a psychologist, and I was working at a large cancer institute and trying to do what psychologists do in providing comfort to people. I think I was doing a reasonably good job. But there was something peculiar that kept emerging, which is that I kept feeling like I was getting more than I was giving. Something very important was happening simply by being there, by taking care of people, by offering them myself, as well as any ideas. It became less psychotherapy or mental-health intervention, less of a job or a career, and more a way of being with people. It didn't seem so discontinuous from the way I wanted to be with everybody in my life, and so I just started to call it something different. I started thinking of it as advocacy. I started thinking of it as service.

Then, when I realized that there was nothing particularly unique about what happened to me, that I could teach other people to enter into the lives of people in need in very much the same way, I saw those early caregivers become inspired in terms of their interest and commitment. I realized that a deep human impulse was getting touched in all of us that had to do with service, and that it was just as strong as self-concern. The philosopher Schopenhauer offered an observation that always struck me at the beginning of my work. Everybody thinks that self-preservation is the deepest, most powerfully embedded of the human drives, but in fact, he said, the need to serve others, to preserve the lives of others, is just as strong as self-preservation. It struck me that way. I've seen that happen when people put their own well-being and peace of mind in jeopardy to serve others. At an even deeper level, there is the realization that self and other are one.

Would you say that there is a goal in your work? Is it goal oriented or is it process oriented?

CHARLES: It's much more process oriented. There are occasionally goals that are important, yet it's much more mission driven than goal driven. I ask myself, "How do I offer the best of myself to another person in a context in which he or she has an identified need, and how do we create together a spiritual partnership that is mutual—that is, a partnership where we both give and we both receive?"

Where would a service like this happen? Does it happen ordinarily in a hospital, in somebody's home?

CHARLES: The work that I'm doing personally would take place through community organizations like Shanti Project and in hospitals, but we're talking about a much larger frame for this. We're talking about the kind of work that people can do anywhere in their lives. In fact, the way Shanti Project happened, was I was at a large cancer institute, trying to care for 40 people who were acutely ill, and there was no way that I could see them all. I had to recruit other folks who we trained to be patient advocates, to be service providers of a different kind and to be available to people who were in need. These early peer counselors did extraordinarily well. The idea took off, and Shanti became a model for other organizations in this country and abroad. The simple idea at the core of it all was that you could train people in the skills necessary to serve a specific population, and also show them how to simply be with another human being. That idea of a compassionate presence is central to caring for people in general. It is central to the widespread network of a compassionate community that Shanti has engendered.

Lynne, how about your work? Would you say it's goal oriented or process oriented?

LYNNE: I would answer almost exactly as Charlie did. It's very mission driven. There's a lot of process in it. If there is a goal, it is transformation of the condition of human life through the window of ending hunger. For example, if you work on ending hunger, and I do mean *ending* it, there is a goal there. If you work on it with some real commitment, which of course I do, and I hope that most of the people I'm working with do, you need to deal with all the major issues of our time, all the great challenges that we face now in history—the emergence of women, cultural and political breakdowns, the relationship with the earth. So you get involved in all the great and wonderful processes that face us as we end this millennium. In that way, it's process oriented, but what makes it so exciting is that we've taken something that was amorphous and sort of inevitable and made it finite, graspable, and resolvable, which is a very exciting way to work on something that has plagued humanity since the beginning of civilization. I must answer, yes, it's both. It's process oriented, and it's very mission driven, and we are working toward a goal of completing one of humanity's most serious and most pernicious enemies.

Would you say in the last 20 years that you've actually seen real progress in eradicating hunger?

LYNNE: Yes. There are many, many ways to answer that question. Hunger is a huge, huge human issue. When you work on hunger, you end up working on many different dimensions of the human condition on a global scale. We have seen progress that was completely unpredictable in parts of the world such as India. I think you probably know that food production in India was not close to enough to feed its population in the '70s. They were a food-deficit nation. Now they export food to Africa. There is progress like that in factual terms.

But I think what's more important and what's more exciting to measure is that the development now has become human centered and focused upon literally empowering people in a way that they are able to become self-sufficient and self-reliant participants on this planet. In that respect, there's just been awesome progress in many parts of the world, which is most exciting. This is what the whole thing is about. The goal of ending hunger is a very real, concrete goal, but what we really are going for is the transformation of the condition of life for people—about a billion of them on the planet today—who actually just don't have a chance. When they have a chance, they always make it. The progress is enormous, in numbers and in facts, and it's also enormous in terms of giving people some real sense of who they are and the fact that they are the authors of their own destiny. I mean, by the hundreds and millions. I think the progress is astounding, and there is a long way to go.

How can someone do this kind of work if they've got real work to do? How does one get involved in something like this when they've got their own work?

CHARLES: Most Shanti volunteers work; they have jobs. They have careers, and yet they volunteer three, six, even ten hours a week or more to take care of people with AIDS, to take care of family members of people with AIDS. And before AIDS, Shanti volunteers cared for people with cancer and their loved ones. A basic question lying at the heart of this work is: What need gets gratified for someone who works hard at a regular job but still feels that something vital is missing? What deep human need get gratified in a project like Shanti or the Hunger Project or any other wonderful service organizations or cause?

Somebody once said that anytime two people meet in America, they form an organization. America is loaded with service-oriented organizations that people can connect with and volunteer their time and expertise to. What I fear is that the general public thinks it is merely more energy expended and more work to do, and somehow it's effortful drudgery. Yet, if you listen to the stories and the lives of the people who have committed in this way to a service advocacy role, they will tell you that some of the most sublime pleasures they ever experience come in the context of their service work. They say you get far more than you give. That certainly is true for me.

Lynne, do you have stories like that, too?

LYNNE: Let me just preface it by saying that I think that people will give up anything to make a difference in their lives. I think that is an unknown secret of humanity. I have found in The Hunger Project that we've had literally tens of thousands of volunteers in countries all over the world. I've seen people with my own eyes who have very significant jobs, like doctors, lawyers, or members of Parliament or significant leaders of major corporations in India, for example, who will put their commitment toward living a life that expresses a stand larger than themselves, before anything else, and it will imbue their job, whatever their job is policeman, fireman, nurse—with a kind of power they were always looking for.

One of my favorite examples is an old Hunger Project story. In the early days, we did everything through volunteers. We had no staff. There was a woman who was a manicurist, and she called up our little office. She said, "I just read about the Hunger Project, and I think it's an outrageous idea to go around talking about ending world hunger, but somehow it's calling to me and I want to do something. But I'm just a manicurist, I don't know anything about hunger, I don't speak any other languages. What can I do?" I said, "Well, the question of the Hunger Project is to ask and answer the question yourself: What can I do? How can I make a difference?" And she was very frustrated with me because I didn't give her envelopes to address, or something concrete to do like going down to some soup kitchen.

In the beginning, we worked to have people find this commitment in themselves, and not just try to sign them up for something. She was very unhappy with our conversation, and told me so. She hung up on me and then called me back a couple days later. She said, "I got it! I got it! I'm going to do a fingernail-painting-athon for the end of hunger." And she did, and I'll tell you it was the most amazing thing. She got the Century Plaza, a big hotel in Los Angeles, to donate a ballroom to her. She got all the manicurist friends she knew. They did a fingernail-painting-athon on a Sunday, all day long, like from nine to nine. They charged something minimal for manicures, but enough to make some money. They all donated their time, and she raised $3,000 for The Hunger Project, and all the manicurists were briefed on ending hunger and inspiring people about what they could do.

So while they were painting people's nails, instead of gossiping about the girl next door, they were actually creating a productive conversation for people to get involved in an issue that this woman cared about. She did this every month for something like two or three years, and it became a huge thing. This was an example of someone taking their own profession and imbuing it with meaning. She didn't have to become something she wasn't. She did not have to suddenly become a world leader. She didn't have to understand something she didn't understand. She just took the commitment that was beginning to build inside of her and found a way to express it in her normal, ordinary life.

That's when I think this is the kind of thing that's most successful for people. They can discover something in their own lives and bring to it a kind of meaning and power and beauty from a stand that they've taken for living their life in a way that matters. That gives people their life, really.

CHARLES: There's so much to say, so many images and so many stories, and I can really empathize with Lynne's task of trying to pick one example. There was a Shanti volunteer who's a masseuse who got a call from another volunteer whose client was dying and who didn't know what the right action would be. We speak frequently of acting from the heart, or intelligent right action, but it isn't always easy to determine such action. In fact, presence matters far more than action in many instances.

Here, the man who was dying had been a classical music afficionado—opera, especially. He hadn't listened to opera in a long time. It just didn't move him anymore. The volunteer/masseuse had this wonderful tape of Maria Callas. She visited the dying man, lit candles, turned down the lights, and the other volunteer put on the tape of Maria Callas just as the massage was starting. The man's tears began to fall as he looked up and said, "I had forgotten how beautiful." Simple action. He talked about how music had been such an important part of his life. Now it could continue to be in the time he had left. He lived two more weeks and listened to his music collection every day during that time, and he died with that same tape of Maria Callas playing in his room.

So if you were to ask, What is the special skill? There wasn't any. The masseuse already knew how to give massages. It was simply two human beings who cared enough to communicate about what the right action might be. When people say, Well, what is your credential for doing this work? The answer is: Your heart is your credential. There was no evolved technical expertise or professional expertise. It used to be called neighborliness. If I had trouble building my house, you would come over with a bunch of other neighbors, and you'd help me build my house, and I'd help you build yours. That's the context we're talking about. That's the essential peer support model. We've been so professionalized in our thinking—George Bernard Shaw said that the professions are a conspiracy against the laity, against the lay public. This is not a knock against professional expertise, but there's a lot that can be offered as basic neighborliness, skilled compassionate work.

Bernard Shaw is an example himself of someone who never went to college. He's probably considered one of the great intellectuals of the 20th century.

CHARLES: Perhaps that's why he had a better perspective on looking at the relationship between the professions and the lay public. My experience with Shanti and many other community-based service organizations teaches me that this notion of citizen advocacy of expecting the best from ourselves and offering it to other people, all the while transforming ourselves in partnership with them, is one of the most rewarding aspects of human life. I don't know what else moves me quite as much as being in a position to offer somebody something that they really need, that they might really benefit from, and by doing so connecting us in a simple process of giving. What was that wonderful quote from Hillel that everybody uses, "If I am not for myself, who will be for me? But if I am only for myself, what am I?" And you know what? Everybody forgets the third line: "And if not now, when?" That's the point—if not now, when?

The main question, then, is when are you going to care? When are you going to sit up and take notice? It seems like it's time to sit up and take notice and to become engaged in something.

LYNNE: When I say the word *hunger,* it conjures up a child who is malnourished or starving. But there's the front and the back side of hunger. There's the front side of the hand of hunger that is the physical condition of about a billion, about one-fifth of us on the planet now. Then there's the back side of the hand of hunger, which is just as serious, probably more serious, which is the hunger for meaning, a hunger to make a difference with one's life, a hunger to find value, to leave the planet better than we found it. That hunger is as deep, and as important, and I consider them all one hunger. One is a reflection of the other.

In order to end physical hunger—or we could take any real problem on earth—it will involve resolving and actually beginning to recognizing and doing something about the spiritual hunger, the hunger of the soul. Mother Teresa said that the hunger in America is the most serious hunger in the world because it's the poverty of the soul. Our society offers volunteer opportunities unlike any country on earth that I've been to. Because we are in an addictive, consumptive set of patterns, we are driven away from a lot of the very things that would nurture us as human beings. I feel very strongly that there isn't anyone on earth today who isn't longing to make a difference with their life, who isn't longing for a way to serve and be useful to others. I think that one of the great conditions that we are facing in the world is that everyone has a contribution to make. What's missing is a space or a way for them to see how to contribute. We need to really get out there and give people these pathways, because it will transform their lives.

Does this type of service relate to a given spiritual practice? Do each of you have a spiritual practice?

CHARLES: For me, the service is the spiritual practice. Yet, it takes different forms. For instance, recently we've been meeting with people in small groups called "wisdom circles," groups of people who talk about their service work, and talk about, in my case, AIDS care-giving. What it's like taking care of people with AIDS, what opens up transformatively for me as an individual, for us collectively, in such a situation. What we are learning in wisdom circles is that there's no separate sense that I do my service work and then I do my spiritual practice. No, they've been all of a piece for a very, very long time. The people we meet with in wisdom circles get a chance to speak from the heart and listen from the heart and engage in deep truth-telling about the impulse and motivation that drives their service work. What I find is that people are almost unanimous in saying that this work is their spiritual path.

Is this the same with you, Lynne?

LYNNE: Yes, very much so. I think the contact I've had, or the great privilege I've had of working with people in the developing world, has given me access to a spiritual way of being. It isn't like a religion or a particular set of meditation techniques or anything. When you hang out with African women or the poorest people in the world for any period of time and you have some access to deep spiritual truths that people who face life and death situations all day, every day, have access to, it has a profound impact on one's life. Before I actually started traveling to these places, I would also answer the question the same way. My work is both my service and access to my spirituality. Somehow if you can find a way in your life to unlock your own calling, by opening yourself to your own calling, in there is the spiritual practice of your life. So I would say, it's all one for me. I also use spiritual practices that I've come upon in the meantime to empower myself, but really, primarily, to be more effective in my work, which is my chosen service to humanity and the planet.

CHARLES: The part I keep thinking about is how we separate so reflexively one thing from another, work from enjoyment, service from career, as if somehow these distinctions are real, rather than something that derives from the values that undergird our society. When you find people becoming more whole, integrating more of their lives, integrating mind and body and spirit, one of the things that you find is that this service becomes more central. It becomes a natural expression of a life well lived. It doesn't become something that you tack on to life. If I had enough time, if I had enough money, when things are better, then maybe I'll do some good work in the world. It becomes a way of being in the world, a natural expression of a more integrated life. I don't mean anything esoteric, and I don't mean anything that's only reserved for a few people. I mean that service work can be a source of immense gratification for all of us.

The Shanti Project started at a point—and I remember it quite well—when many of the early volunteers had very few financial resources to draw upon. This was not a wise career choice for me either. I had just gotten a Ph.D. in psychology, and my friends were accepting all sorts of appointments at prestigious universities or going into private practice, and I was starting a volunteer project. People would ask me, Why in the world are you doing that? I remember thinking, *Real freedom is having no choice*—no choice in the sense that this is exactly what I want to do. How could you ask me to do something other than the perfect thing for me? That perfect thing, that path that motivates each of us more than any other, is there for all of us. Sometimes it manifests quickly, sometimes not. But that kind of sublime fulfillment is there for everybody.

LYNNE: I would say the same thing. I think part of what happens in life is that we do categorize. There's service over here, work over here, family over here, and then people are always struggling with having things get more balanced. I really have an argument with that. When you are living a whole and complete life, or what I would call a committed life, you don't ever have to worry about balancing anything. You don't ever have to worry about keeping your options open because you've surrendered, which is where freedom is located. There is a beautiful quote from a Zen text, and it can be applied to a man, too: *"A woman who is a master of the art in living makes little distinction between her work and her play, her labor and her leisure, her mind and her body, her education and her recreation, her love and her religion. She hardly knows which is which. She simply pursues her vision of excellence and grace in whatever she does, leaving others to decide whether she is working or playing. To her, she is always doing both."*

I would say that when you have really found or allowed yourself to discover that which your life is about, you don't need to work on balance, or keeping this over here and that over there and what about the kids and am I spending too many hours in this, that, or the other thing? You live a life of integrity, which means wholeness and completeness. Everything you do is imbued with the power and beauty of life itself. I know there are a lot of workshops about how to keep it all together and balance it all. And I think it misleads people, because as soon as you've surrendered, it all works out.

When making that surrender, it seems as if one enters what appears to be a field of chaos in some sense. But in going into that field, one realizes that there's a deeper pattern that's very connective in the midst of chaos. Chaos is no longer chaos.

LYNNE: Archimedes said, "Give me a place to stand, and I'll move the world." When you take a stand, it shapes who you are, it sets your priorities, it wakes you up in the morning, it puts you to bed at night. It dresses you.

It helps other people to stand. It's inspiring.

LYNNE: When you take a real profound stand, you join the ranks of Mahatma Gandhi and Martin Luther King—people who lived from a stand. In that space, there is enormous power in the most beautiful sense of the word *power.* A power with a great freedom, and it is a deep spirituality in that way of being. You don't have to think about it. You're not working on your spirituality. You're not working on your transformation. All that disappears, and you become an instrument. It's really a gift to have that opportunity, which every single person on earth has, in my view.

CHARLES: Please understand that daily life is filled with tasks to do and phone calls to make and appointments to keep, and it's filled with things that you'd really like to get accomplished. We're not talking about some kind of unusual life that you wouldn't recognize in terms of how it actually plays out in the course of a day or a week. It's the quality of energy that you bring to those activities, that you bring to that agenda. If you are sitting on the floor licking envelopes and putting stamps on envelopes, but the cause or the activity is something that you are committed to on the highest level of your being, then you are actually fine doing simple tasks. There's not a big deal about serving in that capacity.

In the hierarchical way our organizations are frequently structured, it may be likely that somebody who runs an organization wouldn't be caught dead doing simple tasks. However, if you are talking about service work in the way that we are trying to map out in this conversation, it is entirely appropriate for anybody to contribute in any way that furthers what we are trying to get accomplished. And there often isn't that feeling of drudgery. What would happen if you tried this in the average workplace? Anybody who's got a job in a traditional organization knows that a thousand times a month people feel violated by being asked to do things they feel are beneath them. There is no above and beneath in service. Rather, it's collaborative, it's contributory, it's a partnership. There is so much less of an "us" and "them" involved in it, and much more of simple "us."

Psychologists are now trying to define notions like "eco-self" to describe a way of being in which I incorporate the earth into my identity. I think service work in general is work that incorporates the other into his or her identity. If your end of the boat sinks, so does mine. We are all of a piece. We are connected in a very, very basic way. I don't know how many people had this experience of deep connection when they were young. It seems to me that service-oriented folks frequently learned this lesson early in life.

I grew up in New York, and I remember being taken to Manhattan by my parents. I would see people sitting in the winter in the cold, sometimes amputees with little tin cans, and they wanted some money, and so I would drop in whatever coins I had. Then, I couldn't forget them for the rest of the day. We might be going to the circus or the museum or something, and I'd constantly ask my parents, What happened to the man sitting there? Where does he go at night? What if he doesn't get enough money to eat? I must have been 8 or 9 or 10 years old. I remember thinking at the time how important it was that we go back to see if he's okay, because there was nobody to take care of him.

The point I'm making is that the impulse to care about others is deep. It's a deep impulse even in cultures like ours, where radical individualism, survival of the fittest, who's the top gun, et cetera, is still revered. We lose track of the normalcy of deep connection and collaboration. Through service work we can make a much stronger case for human beings being linked emotionally, spiritually, materially, and psychologically. Our identities include one another and the natural world. This is an identity far healthier than the radical individualist who's trying to prove that he or she is "better than" all others.

You mentioned wisdom circles earlier. Can you tell us more about them?

CHARLES: A wisdom circle is a group of people who meet using a set of constants or guidelines such as speaking from the heart, listening from the heart, and making room for silence to enter to govern their participation. A talking stick is passed, a symbolic object that allows the person speaking while holding the object to be the focus of everyone's heartfelt attention. Everybody else in the room listens to that person talk from direct experience while bearing witness silently to what he or she says.

For instance, in our wisdom circles with AIDS caregivers, you have people who are sitting at the bedsides of seriously ill people, experiencing chronic trauma themselves often for years, and they really had no place to talk about what they experience, including the very, very deep spiritual connections they have with those they serve. The wisdom circle allows these folks to come together in a safe and sacred space and share their truths, their stories. They talk about what happened to them, what they learned, how they feel, and what they want to share with others in the group.

Wisdom circles involve paying attention to others with unconditional love, unconditional positive regard, and listening from the heart. What is key is the safety of the wisdom circle, as opposed to other groups where there's a lot of cross-talk and interruption and analysis and arguments abounding at times. In a safe space, people are willing to share their truths more fully, to tell what they experienced so that others can bear witness. When you consider very arduous situations like an AIDS pandemic, people go through extraordinary stress in the service of other human beings. For years I've called it enlightenment at gunpoint. You may be learning incredible amounts, but in the roughest of situations. Where do you process your experiences? Whom do you tell your stories to and have them listen from the heart?

And that's essentially what the wisdom circle is—a safe and sacred space for a group of people to gather, to listen and speak from the heart. We're very committed now to teaching others to convene wisdom circles, and to share their truths with kindred spirits.

I guess the circle, the gathering of small groups of people, has been around for millennia.

CHARLES: It's ancient, and no matter what culture you come from, if you push the lineage back far enough, you realize that your ancestors sat around a fire telling stories.

We're fond of saying that here at New Dimensions we're sitting around the spray of microphones telling stories for the New Dimensions radio shows. The difference is that we don't have a fire.

CHARLES: We have the benefit of you as an interviewer. We have the sense of having done this storytelling before, of being accomplished at it. And perhaps millennia ago, our forefathers felt very accomplished at this form of gathering, also. What the ancient cultures knew that we are just starting to rediscover is that the stories shared were absolutely indispensable for the health and cohesion of the collective, for the tribe to continue and for the individual and the collective to prosper. We are rediscovering the importance of sharing our stories in a circle and having other people witness our truths.

Somewhere a long time ago in a distant galaxy, we all agreed to do this again, and here we are. Lynne, you take people who have volunteered or have given funding to support some of the projects you are involved in, and you take them out to the countryside. I know you've taken a group to Bangladesh and to Africa. What about the paradox of coming from a country like the United States, which is very wealthy and very rich, and you travel to another country that is much less so. Some people are shocked with that kind of paradox. How does that work?

LYNNE: I usually take our largest donors (I don't mean physical size, but in terms of the amount of money they've given), to the poorest places on earth. Bangladesh is the second poorest country in the world. Mozambique is the poorest country in the world. It has that nonenviable distinction. But when people in our part of the world go to these places—and not like tourists—we meet with and spend time with the people who are facing the conditions of hunger and poverty that are so harsh and so severe that they need more courage to live through one day than any of us will need in our lifetime. What happens is that a partnership forms. People in our part of the world stop feeling sorry for, or badly about, the conditions in which many others are living. Instead, they have enormous respect and are deeply moved by these people. The harsh conditions in which they live forges them into a kind of courageous being that has some real lessons to teach those of us who don't live in those kinds of circumstances. These trips are very harsh.

You're not staying at the Hyatt Regency.

LYNNE: No, we're not, and it's hot, and everybody has malaria, and there are flies, and there's no place to go to the bathroom, et cetera. You can imagine. Part of what that does is forge a partnership. (There are 5.8 billion people on the planet now, and 4.6 billion of us live in developing countries. Only 1.2 billion of us live in the Western or Northern industrialized societies, so we are clearly in the minority. We're 20 percent, and then people in the developing world are 80 percent of humanity. And if we really, truly want a global society and we must have one, and we are beginning to see one, we can no longer live in isolation of the 4.6 billion people.) In my view, I would say that the 300 million poorest women in the world are the keepers of the wisdom that will give us all a sustainable future. Meeting these people and being together and holding hands and embracing and sitting around the fire together and staying in the same village together and really talking about the human problems we face, alters people so fundamentally that we have a lot harder time coming back than going. Entering into this society, with very heavily driven addictive, consumptive patterns, it's offensive to come home. People get a little righteous. And you know, we need to help them readjust to this part of the world. You see, we have our own horrors. Resource-poor people obviously have enormous challenges and are trapped in vicious cycles; the dowry system in India, for example. Some of these things are really not serving anyone. But we have our own vicious cycles. We're trapped in an affluent society that has its own blindness, traps, and addictions. We need compassion for ourselves as well. So that's some of what happens to people on these journeys. They go very deep and see their lives and their world in new ways. It's very, very powerful work.

EPILOGUE

Gandhi said, "Be the change you want to see in the world." Both Lynne Twist and Charles Garfield personify Gandhi's admonition and show us how each of us can make a profound difference in the world. It is through service that we can express compassion for the other, who is a reflection of us. What's important to remember is that we can make a commitment from where we stand right now. It requires nothing other than our willingness to make a difference in whatever way feels right for us.

✦ CHAPTER THREE ✦

Discovering Soul
in the Workplace

David Whyte and Michael Toms

PROLOGUE

*W*ork can mean more than simply earning an income. It
can also serve as a tempering element to articulate a life
truly worth living. Challenges abound in the corporate world as
we now face a dramatically changing marketplace. More than
ever, businesses will need people of vision and creativity to
survive. How can we learn to navigate these dangerous waters,
maintaining both our jobs and our humanity? Where can we find
strength in creativity to help us take the risks necessary to grow
and prosper?

The interest in the works of Joseph Campbell, the extraordinary success of Scott Peck's The Road Less Traveled, and best-
sellers by Robert Bly and Jungians Thomas Moore and Clarissa
Pinkola Estes strongly indicate that many of us are actively

*searching for a more meaningful existence. David Whyte is some-
body who is working actively to enrich the way we view ourselves
and our work and what we do with our lives.*

*David grew up in the hills and valleys of Yorkshire, England,
and now lives on an island in the state of Washington. He's worked
extensively within corporate America, bringing an understanding
of the process of change through an innovative use of poetry. His
clients include many Fortune 500 companies. He is the author of*
The Heart Aroused: Poetry and the Preservation of the Soul in
Corporate America, *four books of poetry, an audiocassette lecture
series, and an album of poetry and music.*

MICHAEL TOMS: *David, how did the transition occur for
you from writing poetry, to writing a book about corporate
America and the soul?*

DAVID WHYTE: It happened in the best American fashion.
I was giving a keynote talk at a conference in 1987, and after the
talk a stranger came up to me and said, "We have to hire you." I
said, "For what?" And he said, "To come into corporate America
and work with some of the issues we're working with right now."
I had an initial, strong wave of skepticism about it because I had
an inherited prejudice about corporations and the work they did in
the world. The man turned out to be Peter Block, who's a very
well-known author, philosopher, and business consultant. He
wrote a book called *The Empowered Manager* and has a new book
called *Stewardship*. Really, he was uncovering qualities and
themes in his workshops that were beyond the normal ideas of
what it meant to be a corporate manager. They were basically
entering timeless realms of human experience, and they were
going where the poet treads more easily, in a way. So they wanted
me to speak to these fears, griefs, and losses—fiery experiences

that were appearing when they really took the work to its logical conclusions. They were asking people: What is your real vision in the workplace? And what is your real passion?

When you set these ideals against most organizations and most places where we work, we find, as Joseph Campbell said, that you have your ladder against the wrong wall. Not only that you've had your ladder for years against the wrong wall, but that you've also been inlaying gold leaf into this ladder. So I was invited in. I expected to be at least a little corrupted by corporate America, but I was intrigued enough to want to do it. My work has been, and is about, bringing poetry back into the mainstream and having people understand how incredibly precise it is about the human adventure—and how it can tell you about the phenomenology of the path—in other words, what happens along the way.

I was just astonished by the openness and the enthusiasm for the work. What I found was that there was an incredible pragmatism and practicality in that world and, in fact, people are so desperate now because all the old structures are falling away that anything that really works for them in helping to understand human relationships, they will take hold of. So, there is an astonishing openness which, for instance, isn't there in academia. It's not there in the universities. The university has its own world laid out as they want it to be. But in some ways, the corporate world is very open right now, very vulnerable, too. And it's at a marvelous place for transformation, in a really practical sense.

Certainly in the United States, there is a whole movement. It's small, but it's building. Businesses and corporations have decided that they are going to do business as if people mattered. The bottom line or the profit is directly related to how well they serve people and work with people. I think of the magazine Business Ethics. *Corporations like Ben and Jerry's Ice Cream; Tom's of Maine, with natural products; and Celestial Seasonings tea have been very successful as organizations and also have been successful in serving people. There does seem to be a building movement in corporate America in this direction.*

There is. I would take another step from that conversation. I feel that ethics are not enough right now. Ethics, in some ways, are conceptual structures, another way of being that comes out of an abstracted sense of what is good and right. What I'm trying to work with in my book, *The Heart Aroused*, are the urgencies of the soul in the workplace. It's my opinion that the soul will break every taboo to live its life in the world, including kill, if it's forced into that corner. And there is an astonishing passion and urgency inside each human being that causes tremendous destruction if it is not addressed.

Our creative energies turn quickly destructive if not given a framework to support them. The very thing in the workplace, in the American workplace at least, that the corporations are asking for, is creativity and adaptability on the part of the people. They are asking for that because they won't survive if they don't have it. The market has changed. A whole industry can disappear overnight now. You cannot legislate creativity in the workplace. You cannot say, I want an increase in the creativity quotient of 8.75 percent this week, rising to a plateau of 9 percent. It doesn't work. The request is absurd. Why? Because common sense tells us that creativity and adaptability belong to the passion and enthusiasm of a person, and their passions belong to their souls. And their souls love the fiery experiences that bubble at the center of life more than they love the company, and so the very thing corporations have to do is to invite the part of the person that does not belong to the company into the company. We have to take the part of us that does not belong to the work *into* the work, and that's the only way we are going to be able to anything new in our work to move forward.

In the 1960s, I was in corporate America and worked for a multinational corporation. It feels like a previous incarnation. The business was compartmentalized. There was business, and there was the family, and there was the spiritual. The spiritual area, the soul area, and the family area were distinctly separate from the business, and the business took precedence. It was the priority that if the business requested it, you needed to move across the country. It didn't matter that the family was uprooted and all of that. That wasn't really a consideration. Do you find that that kind of compartmentalization exists in some of the corporations you work with?

It does, but it's receding and has to change, because if you want a whole person in your office, you don't want them split and pulled in many different directions. The old contract was, in the words of Peter Block, sacrifice now for future unstated promises.

That's right. And some of them were even stated. I remember when I left my corporation that there was great consternation among the management because I was leaving this career position after eight years, and there were people there who said, How can you do this...you're giving up a pension, and so on. Well, as it turned out, some years later, maybe ten years after I left, the company went bankrupt, and these people lost all that they had been promised.

Those promises were always delusionary, in a sense, although they were followed through enough to make sure that the delusion never completely popped over the years. Now, increasingly, almost no one can keep the promises that were made, not even IBM, which promised that they would never have layoffs. Individual people would be let go, but there would be no massive layoffs. And there was so much betrayal once layoffs began in that organization around the parental matrix that had been created.

So much of our experience is predicated on the parent–child relationship. Especially in the workplace. So if I act in a childlike manner and do as I'm told and don't rock the boat, you, as parent, will take care of me. Well now, the parents are saying, Look, we can't take care of you in that way. Not because we don't want to. But we can't. It's too expensive for us, and things change too much. We need you to be a mature adult. Now sometimes it's actually the employees who are saying that to the company. It works both ways. Sometimes the company doesn't want anything to do with that. But quite often a company will decide it has to change, and then all the individual members including the people who are the executives suddenly realize the consequences of what they are actually speaking about. Because when you are talking about facing the world as a mature adult, you are talking about letting go of your parking space, you're talking about a different pay structure, you're talking about eliminating levels in the organization so there is more free flow of information, and people can actually treat one another as peers.

I want to go back to the roots of why this has been this way. Again, I want to draw on my own experience and my own family. My roots are in Ireland. My great-grandparents came from Ireland, and my grandfather worked for the Bureau of Engraving and Printing for 45 years. This is where they make paper money in America. My grandmother worked for the telephone company for 44 years. So they had this one job most of their adult life. And of course they couldn't understand anyone not having a career position like that. So when I left, it was very confusing to them. But I see where they came from. Their parents came from Ireland and had no work. No place to work. And they came to America to get work. So work was very, very important to them. Getting a career position was extremely important to them. They could feel secure in having a job for the rest of their life, and they didn't have to worry about it. In some sense, at that stage of the evolu-

tion of the United States, there were lots of people in that position, as well as corporations that grew up around that idea and that focus. Then it got out of balance later. One can see the history of how it happened.

There was tremendous hope for safety, which came out of the Depression. People were scarred by that experience, and so there was a wonderful comfort to this marvelous parental structure that would take care of you and your children and your health so long as you just put your feet in the right place. The urgencies of the soul, I feel, are so strong in our time now that they will come out in whatever way they can. Just because we happen to be earning a living is no excuse for not following the life that you feel might be possible for you. I feel like somehow there has been an increase in the pressure around our destinies.

The flame has been increased.

Yes, I think we all realize that we are affecting life, increasingly. That we may affect our collective survival through our own virtuous efforts. The intuitive feeling is that human beings can upset the balance of life and destroy everything, and that the stakes are very high, and that's reflected in an individual life. You can have a tragic life—not by failing, but by living out someone else's life. That is the ultimate death to the soul. The soul would much rather fail at its own life than succeed at someone else's. So far, much of corporate America has involved succeeding at other people's lives, living out other people's images, whether it's through the career track or through advertising or whatever. Now there is a feeling that no matter how large the organization, it is not large enough for even one human soul. It's just not big enough to hold the longing, the vision, and the particularity of each life, and that somehow we need to make our organizations much smaller. I think we need to make them so small that they are actually just one person. This does not mean we would not work together in command systems, but that I would not work for an organization at all costs.

Eventually, the feeling would be that you have mature individuals who are ready to move on and go through transitions. A good sign to me of a healthy company is that the people you have employed with you could just pick up and go and set up in opposition if they wanted. Then you know you have a real peer relationship. Then you know you are working creatively at the edge of what you are about. Then you know the right people are in the room, and less of the structure is based around safety. Less of it is based around future promises. More of it is based around another new kind of loyalty, which has to do with a primary first-hand engagement with life.

In speaking about waking up to one's passion and finding out what one's calling is, how does one awaken to that passion inside an organization where one is essentially working in a job, and so forth? How does that work?

In some ways, it works in the same way that it has always worked throughout the millennia for human beings. In outwardly difficult and impossible situations, you must speak your life. You must take the first steps into the unknown. As Joseph Campbell has said: "In the beginning of the path, if you can see it laid out before you, then you know it's not your path, it's someone else's that you mistook for your own." The corporation is simply a kind of outer structure of our own internal bureaucracy. All the reasons why we immobilize ourselves are present there in this outer structure. The corporation is simply a body, literally a corpus of people who have come together to do things that are impossible to do alone. And there is something marvelous about that. So the question is: How can you live out your own individual path within that corporation? I'm not talking about that now just from the point of selfishness; I'm actually talking about it from the selfless ability to be able to give your true gift to the world. If you haven't followed your own path, you can't.

Sometimes you may be able to do it within the corporation, and sometimes you really need to leave.

Yes. But the initial temptation is that the grass is always greener. So you give it at least three good-faith attempts in that place to know whether this is real or right for you.

What about the phenomenon of what's being called entrepreneuring in corporations, where corporations are recognizing that there are very creative people in their midst who are employees that want to do their own thing, so they create these little pockets to allow them to explore their own creativity within the structure.

Eventually we have to get to the point where we don't see them as pockets, where we are actually starting to build them into our relationships. All of the structures now are breaking down— our governments, our nations, our understandings of marriage and what that means over time, and our workplaces. When the Berlin Wall fell, we intuitively knew that the nearest thing we had to an Eastern European dictatorship was a Western corporation —those revolving doors we went through in the morning where you are told this is not a democracy. And the contract was to be taken care of, as long as you did what you were told. The world of business cannot stand that because it simply doesn't work anymore. There's someone producing something twice as fast as you—and more creatively—and the world of the individual cannot stand it anymore because people are literally dying on their feet, standing over their computer terminals, living out other people's lives. This is where the ethics question will not take us far enough. Because the urgencies of the soul are so powerful, there are very fiery conversations that have to be had when you start exploring these things—

fiery conversations with yourself and with others about what the real relationships are.

Your book The Heart Aroused *deals with bringing poetry into the corporation. One of the chapters in the book had Beowulf as a model. Perhaps you could talk about that.*

I work with poetry as a way of understanding change in the corporation, so I have hundreds of poems memorized. Beowulf is one of those poems that I use as a way of illustrating that you are not exempt from these ancient human explorations of the dark side of existence. When I say dark side, I mean the waning side, the part that we would rather not have there, but which we have to deal with every day. Actually, when I am working in the corporate world, I say tongue in cheek, that Beowulf is basically a sixth-century consultant because he was an Anglo-Saxon prince who hired his services out to distant kings and princes who needed his work. He had turned up on the shores of Denmark offering to rid the king of this terrible monster, which came out in the middle of the night after the ring-giving and feasting was over. It fought off the best warriors and dragged off young men and women to the swamp, where it ate them, and the name of this monster was Grendel. This is a perfect, very precise description.

It's all very well in the evening when "employee of the month" plaques are being handed out to the worthy. But at two in the morning when you really have to face your life as you are living it, then something larger, hidden and more urgent appears and grabs the innocent part of you back to the swamp. And you can think of grief being where you decide to go down and work with that yourself, go down and confront Grendel. Depression is where Grendel comes up and grabs you anyway and pulls you down, and you don't know why you have this kind of subterranean pressure around you all day.

But there's a description of the lake in the poem, and I recite this to engineers and salespeople and executives and line managers and workers. They all get it. They all understand. The great thing about the story is actually what comes after Beowulf defeats Grendel. They have more feasting, and Beowulf is given all the accolades and the gold. But that night as he sleeps in another hall with his men, something else comes out of the swamp—drags off young men and women, fights off the best warriors—Grendel's mother! The thing you fear is the mother of the thing you fear— it's what gave birth to your fears and your distance and your alienation in the first place.

The ancient bard is saying, You think this is just a story? Don't kid yourself. It is not far from here, nor is it a pleasant spot. And this image of the stag, which is an ancient kind of masculine image, almost male courage in a way—even the stag will not enter the lake. It would rather be torn apart by the dogs on the shore. There is something that is frightening to us about the very place we have to go to find our lives. It's the darkest part of the forest. It's the darkest part of the lake, but it's exactly the place we have to explore.

Our hope is that because we have this marvelous professional environment, we can finesse this experience. The fact is that today we spend more time in the workplace than we do in our churches. We spend more time in the workplace than we do with our families. And we spend more time in the workplace than we do in the natural world. If we decide that we are not going to follow out our destinies in the workplace, we are in a very bad way. Because so much of our life and destiny is lived out in that place. How do you go into the lake and confront the very monstrous difficulties that seem to be preventing you from living out your true life? In the Beowulf chapter in the book, I try to show that you do this whatever way you can. In some work environments, if you are very lucky, you can actually have the conversation. In most workplaces, you have one or two people who you can have that conversation with. Sometimes you don't have anyone. You do it on the plane between Cincinnati and New York with that stranger who you've never met and you will never see again. But somehow you do have the conversation even if it's with yourself. You start at what you are really afraid of, and you start to look at how many of the ostensibly practical forms that are in the corporation are simply the forlorn human hopes for total safety.

Joseph Campbell used to talk about the metaphor of the Round Table and the knights leaving the round table to go in search of the grail. The knights left the round table and entered the forest at the darkest place where there was no path.

That's right, and this is exactly where Dante began the *Comedia*, one of the great epics of Western literature. He wrote: *"In the middle of the road of my life, I awoke in a dark wood."* This is a real place to start—the place where you wake up in your life, and you look at it as if you've just entered your body. You may say, My God, what or who has taken all this time to construct a life that no one would want, least of all myself? Most of us come to that dark part of the wood.

We are discovering our own soul force, and the soul force speaks to us and literally forces us to move in a new direction. Here in the United States, particularly, we've been trained and conditioned so much. Then we discover, maybe early in adulthood or midway in adulthood, that we may be living somebody else's life. We have been so entrained and so enculturated and so conditioned in a way that we really have been living something that's outside of us, that was told to us.

Again, this is a timeless path, and luckily within the poetic tradition, there's a lot of advice. Actually, I should say there is a lot of experience, because a poem, when it is fully inhabited by the body and the voice, is not about an experience; it is the experience itself.

If you want to walk into many of the points along the path and get an indication of what is actually occurring, you can look at poetry. So one of the difficulties, you see, is: How do I choose my own life without being selfish? How do I follow my own path without saying, Devil, take the rest of the world? The way you do it, according to the poetic tradition, is you follow your own internal imagery, but you never take your eyes off the world while you're doing it.

In poetry, for instance, if you take your eyes off the world, then you start writing confessional poetry. Your own experience becomes the arbiter of reality, instead of what is truly real about soul, which is all about meeting. You don't really know what your soul is until you meet the world, because your soul has something to do with patterning. And when I say "pattern," I mean four-dimensional depth, the whole way we are in the world. When you think about it, there have been 15 billion years of evolution. And there are no other people on the whole earth like the four of us here in this studio, for instance. What I feel happens is the world says to us, We've had 15 billion years of evolution, and there is no other part of creation that can fail like you can fail, and you are quibbling. You will not take a step because you are afraid of failing, and yet you are the only part of the universe that can fail in that way. Why quibble? It's your failure. That's your pattern.

That's what is so frightening to us about the soul, because we've had all our eggs in the basket of the strategic mind, which is constantly looking for safety. And the soul is constantly trying to make a break for freedom. It will try to make it through its work. It will try and make it through its voice, through its artistry, through its relationships, its family that it creates around it. Whatever the workplace is, especially in North America since the obsession around work is so total, it is the place where the soul must make or break for freedom.

In 1988, The Power of Myth *was first broadcast on PBS in America, with Bill Moyers and Joseph Campbell. That series was later rebroadcast in the next few years. It made Joseph Campbell almost a household word in American homes, and many people discovered him and his work at that time. One of the things he talked about was following your bliss. Since then, there has been a great deal of misunderstanding about following your bliss, both from critics writing about it and people attempting to understand it. The idea of following your bliss as it relates to doing just what you want to do is fine and great and happy. Yet Campbell said, "When one follows your bliss, the path leads downward." And, of course, people miss that point. There were many critics who missed it and talked about how Campbell was speaking about self-indulgence and self-gratification and just do what you want. What is your view?*

I like Michael Meade's understanding of this word, *bliss*. The derivation of the word comes from the same word as the French word *blessure,* which means "wound." There is something right about this, because your bliss is literally the place where you are open to the world—whether or not you want to be open in that way. Just as when you have a son or daughter, and no matter what the behavior of that son or daughter, it may be wounding to you, but you are open to them. You have no choice. You belong.

I think it is the same way with our own destiny. There are certain ways in which we are vulnerable and open to the world, in which we can do nothing about it. It is both your greatest gift, since it's how you literally flow out into the world, and it's your greatest wound at the same time. It's a place where you do not have ultimate control because you don't have total say over it. The world has as much say, because there's a flow backwards and forwards; in fact, in that place you cannot tell where the world begins and where you start. That's the joy and that's the bliss, and the hope is that you recognize that, and this is true of East or West. The East has just as much difficulty with all these phenomena that we are talking about here as the West does. In the East, the

Buddhist phrase around taking the middle way is often misinterpreted, and the feeling is interpreted the same way as the Golden Rule is in Christian thought. The middle way being, you don't go to any extreme, and you live out this kind of middle ground.

When you try to do that, you find a kind of blandness that knows nothing of either, and the hope is that you can cut your grief off on one side, and the joy will blossom on the other, but it doesn't work, because it's actually the same experience. They are two sides of the same experience. You cut your joy off, and the whole experience shrinks a little more into the middle. You cut your grief off, and it shrinks again. Eventually we are left with something that's really not anything you could term *soul* or the *richness of soul*. Somehow, the middle way really is more like understanding a violin string that is pulled between two points, up to concert pitch, and so you feel grief and you feel joy to the depths.

Our tragedy is that we are always choosing between the two. The ancient tradition, the poetic tradition, says you live out your life between those two points, and that's your bliss, caught right between grief and joy, in the middle.

The burden of human experience at the moment is, or at least the way we've acculturated it, is that we're constantly wanting to be the music notes. So all the notes get pushed together until we have just a bland 60-cycle hum. Which is like an old rusty refrigerator—you only notice when it switches itself off. You say, My God, here's silence, and I don't know what to do with it.

I think it probably comes from the Western Christian work ethic of the goal-oriented job. There is some goal to reach, and so when we apply it to work, particularly if we are trying to follow our bliss, there is some "there" to get to. There is someplace to get to that, Oh, are we there yet? Is everything working? This poem suggests that it's never always working perfectly.

Yes. Time to rest between two notes that are somehow always in discord. That's a true poet. The bad poet would say, My life is a symphony or your life is a symphony, and half of you has to leave the room in order to say that. (By the way, that was a marvelous translation by Robert Bly. You should always mention the translator, as well as the author.)

Our life is constantly being lived out between two worlds. This is a real key to the understanding. And you don't choose either one. It's not so much an iron hands-on experience. It's more like a paintbrush. A way of evoking an experience. I grew up in a household in Yorkshire in the north of England. My father was practical and earthy, wonderful, warm, but very, very practical, and he says a spade is a spade. My mother is Irish. A spade can be anything you want it to be depending on what story you are telling. I lived in this house where the two worlds collided. My father had one clock for all the things he had to do. My mother had a clock for each thing, and each was set at a different time. So if she wanted to catch the number 11 bus, she had one clock five minutes fast. If she wanted to catch the number 3 bus, she had one ten minutes slow. She'd miss the bus if she didn't use the right clock. They were different times interceding.

I became a poet trying to make sense of these two worlds in some ways. I understood intuitively when I was a child that our human tragedy is the fact that we actually choose between these two worlds. And we don't understand that there is a place for the one clock, and there's a place for the many clocks. Unfortunately, all our eggs have gone into the basket of the one clock. In the United States today, we are actually corroding away our ability to have a celebratory experience of life because we are spending so much time that is only demanding one dimension of us. My feeling is not to take yourself completely out of that one dimension. That's one answer. What I am trying to say in *The Heart Aroused* is to bring all your dimensions into the workplace. I am saying this is of tremendous benefit to the corporation and the organization if they can only see it. You may have to leave and go to another one that will be more grateful for your bringing those other dimensions. There is a marvelous opportunity and confluence now, because the very things that the corporations need to survive are actually held in those other more mutable, artistic, poetic, inspirational, and creative dimensions. They are not held in the one dimension in which we've tried to hold everything in place. Their very survivability depends on it.

So it is a wonderful time of opportunity. Poetry, and all the other arts, are of marvelous use in our understanding of how you integrate these other dimensions into the workplace. It's a great moment for the business health of the companies, but it's an even greater moment for our soul's satisfaction and celebration in the world.

There was something you wrote in The Heart Aroused *that says: "Work has to do with cornering and controlling conscious life. It attempts concrete goals. It loves the linear and the defined. But the soul finds its existence through a loss of control to those powers greater than human experience." This is the dilemma many people face.*

I think this again comes back to intuitive understanding in the literate tradition. In some ways, we are always complaining that we don't have the native traditions alive in the tradition of eldership, where these things are taught. But we do, actually. It's in our literate tradition. Our elders are Wordsworth, Coleridge, Emily Dickinson. And we have an astonishing heritage there. And they happen to write in a form in which the experience is totally alive. If you learn how to read poetry on the page and off the page, you can actually evoke Emily Dickinson's heartbeat in the moment of her writing. And the teaching is all there. The experience is all there. (Tell me what was your question; I just got caught in a lyrical flight of fancy there about the use of the poetic tradition.)

It has to do with giving the power over that comes from the personality, the power that comes from the soul. This wanting to control life and work.

If you look at all the understandings around power in the contemplative traditions and the mythic traditions, you find that the ultimate initiation, your ultimate learning about power, always comes through powerlessness. When you are ready for the final teaching about power, it will come through being put in a totally powerless position. If we understand this, we can start short-circuiting, or at least we don't have to go through the final awful steps where we aggrandize power in the American workplace through the corner office, the desk of the pension plan, the stock offering. And then we don't even know who the stock is being given to when we receive it. We don't know who's getting that money, who's getting those benefits. Who has the car? Who has the house? You can start to integrate the experience of power-lessness into your everyday life. You can start to integrate it in a delicious way because you realize that in your own destiny you are giving yourself over to something much greater than you can articulate.

Destiny is always beckoning uncertainty. In some ways, it's more like a gravitational pull. You never arrive there. You just feel yourself come alive in that magnetism. And when you do that, everything else takes a second seat. You can think of the executive driving down the freeway in a kingfisher-blue Porsche. In one way, it's to say, Well, look, the world's going to hell in a handbasket, and here you are in your Porsche, you're burning up the miles. We can wag the finger at the person, and it really doesn't do any good at all, because it's really the soul's attempt to get true celebration through the kingfisher-blue Porsche. The ancient way is to actually evoke the soul's longings in that person, and once that is evoked, the outer trappings are seen for what they are, which is simply secondary.

For instance, when I worked with voice, I began uncovering qualities in the voice. The voice is a window to the soul, and I was working with this fellow one day with his voice, and we finally got to this sound, which was missing from his voice completely. It was a low kind of purring roar. We finally started to work with it, and as we did, as he was making this sound, he said, "I'm a collector of classic cars. This is exactly the sound that they all make." He suddenly realized that the reason he had these things around was to bring this marvelous kind of panther purring roar into his life, which was totally missing. Now once he'd understood this, he did not have to go through a big thing of letting those cars go. It was nothing to him. He doesn't have any of them now, and it wasn't a big thing of, Oh my God, you know, I'm going to follow the spiritual path; therefore, I've got to give up what is dear to me. No, it was like a moment of hilarity: Oh, of course! I've been spending all these hundreds of thousands of dollars on this thing because of this one central, textural experience that is missing from the center of my life.

I thought it was a marvelous moment.

One of the things you mentioned in the book was something that came out of chaos theory, the "strange attracters." What are the strange attracters, relative to work and soul?

That comes out of the chapter called "Coleridge and Complexity," where I'm trying to show that many of the phenomena that are being uncovered in post-modern science, around chaos and complexity, are exactly the things that the poetic tradition have been dealing with for thousands of years. A pattern is not a solid, immobile structure. It actually takes form over time, but it has its own boundaries. You cannot say, however, where those boundaries are at one point. If you look at it over time, you will see the boundaries very clearly. I'm trying to show that instead of trying to exercise iron control over individuals in the workplace, you build teams in which you start to get a feeling for what the strange attracter is. The strange attracter is the name for that pattern over time.

Let's say you have a pendulum and it makes a pattern. Then you give it a knock one minute and you let it swing backwards and forwards and you hit it two minutes later. It will have a strange attracter from those impulses. If you can think of a work team together, the parameters of their movement have to do with their individual characters, with the amount of power and autonomy they have and with the parameters of the job (what they have to do). It also has to do with their creativity. Instead of trying to tell them that this is what you do in every moment for every exigency, you start to look at the pattern, and you have them look at their own pattern, and they find what they are really good at. The worries are that a work team will go off on its own and just spin off the edge of the cliff. But mostly you find that if the parameters are very strong, and the communication is very strong about what the work is about, that they will form their own pattern around that, and that's the strange attracter. It's a very fancy term for something that's mostly intuited and perceived on a daily basis. We just don't have a name for it. Modern science has a name for it.

I would imagine that the corporate executives who bring you into their corporations had to be fairly courageous, because you are coming in there, and doing this work is bound to cause some people to question their jobs and move on to something else.

I try not to put it in that context. My work has to do with living out our life and destinies within that workplace, and it's always tempting to think that the grass is greener elsewhere. I work within the context of actually applying it to transforming the work in which you are in now. Most of them actually are emboldened by the work. Now and again they will try it in the workplace, and it's just so obvious that this is not the place. There are so many other reasons, too, and they leave.

I had a manager at AT&T who basically transformed himself out of a job, because when you really follow this work, you start to understand that the manager is actually a tax on the line worker, and if you really devolve power throughout the organization, the lineworkers are going to decide what management services they want, if they've been educated fully into the business. When you suddenly realize in a very frightening way that your job as a manager is to do yourself out of business or at least to get so near the work that you stop looking at the distinctions between managing and working, now that's very frightening for someone whose mother and father congratulated them because they started work at AT&T, and they knew they had a job for life. The career track was laid ahead of them. It was very courageous of this man who worked with these empowerment issues to such a point that in all conscience he had to leave the organization—not because there was something wrong with the organization, but because his work was being done by others in that particular level. He is now an individual consultant who takes his own gifts into organizations that actually need them now. There is something right about that.

I realize I am referring to Joseph Campbell a lot, but he certainly was one of my mentors. I remember him being asked the question about the search for meaning in life. And he said: "It's not the search for meaning; it's the wanting to feel alive." He also said, "We're not looking for meaning; we're looking for experience," and "It is through the experience and the living of life fully that we experience the divine mystery."

We spend too much time in the workplace these days, not to have that occur there.

You're suggesting in bringing the soul into the workplace to have that experience and to realize it is present if we can really fully experience our aliveness.

Yes. You have to understand that when you are having that difficult conversation with your boss, you are not simply working out a logistical problem. In the presence of that all-knowing authority, that life-or-death control over your wage, your mortgage, car payments and future, that the soul is actually trying to make a break for its own life and destiny in the presence of that authority figure. Through the voice, your soul will be attempting to walk back into your life in the very place where it walked out in the first place. Because usually we gave up our powers to an authority figure, and so the soul is looking for the same experience in order to re-enact and to go through the very doorway it walked out. We wonder why we keep re-creating these experiences where we have the same kind of boss wherever we go or the same kind of peer relationships. I work with this in the chapter "Fire in the Voice," on speaking out at work. The soul is desperate to reconstitute its own life by speaking out its desires in the presence of those to whom we gave it away in the first place.

EPILOGUE

David Whyte reminds us that life is meant to be engaged fully, and this includes work and the workplace. No matter how difficult or challenging the situation may appear to be, we can rest assured that it represents an opportunity to experience our aliveness and to touch our soul life. In their quest for the Holy Grail, the knights of the Round Table "entered the forest at its darkest point, where there was no path." Each entered the darkness of their own soul's journey to discover whatever wisdom would await them on their ultimate quest, just as we do each day that we encounter problems and the unknown in our daily work.

✦ CHAPTER FOUR ✦

Work, Passion, and the Life of Spirit

Matthew Fox, with Michael and Justine Toms

PROLOGUE

*M*ost of us spend one-third of our lives at work. Many of us find ourselves doing more of it and liking it less. A recent national survey suggested that 80 percent of Americans are unhappy in their jobs. Internationally, the figure is 90 percent. What is it that has produced this nearly universal malaise with work? The answer to this question serves as the focus of this chapter.

Matthew Fox is the internationally known author of 15 books that have sold over 700,000 copies and have been translated into seven languages. Some of his titles include Creation Spirituality, Original Blessing, The Coming of the Cosmic Christ, *and a book entitled* The Reinvention of Work: A New Vision of Livelihood for Our Times. *Matthew holds a master's degree in philosophy and theology from Aquinas Institute, and a doctorate in spirituality from the Institute Catholic de Paris. Editor-in-chief of* Creation Spirituality *magazine, he was silenced by the Vatican in 1988 and later dismissed from the Dominican order in 1993. Since then, he has become an ordained Anglican priest, and in 1996 founded the University of Creation Spirituality as a new model of learning for the 21st century.*

MICHAEL TOMS: *Matthew, I think a good place to start is to talk about the difference—as you described in your book* The Reinvention of Work—*between having a job and having work.*

MATTHEW FOX: I think a job is something that carries us over to help pay our bills, but I think work is really why we are here. The key to work, I think, is that the heart gets affected by it. Joy is part of it. I remember a few months ago I was doing a book signing in Washington D.C., and a woman told a story. She had a job for several years and she realized it was really draining her soul and she was dragging herself to the job. But she didn't have another job on the horizon, so she was scared to quit. Finally, just one day she couldn't take it anymore. She knew it was killing her, so she quit. Two months later, she found a job that was also her work, and she said she'd never been so happy in her whole life.

Notice what had happened. First she had to quit her job to be ready for the work, to be vulnerable, and she had to take that risk. It is interesting because it shows that not only is our work part of our spiritual journey, but quitting our work is part of our spiritual journey. It took the courage and the trust of the Universe, on her part, to quit her job, in order to find her work.

MICHAEL: *This brings up a salient issue for many people, and that is how difficult it is to quit a job because one feels locked* *in to it. One may have life insurance, health insurance, a retirement plan, et cetera.*

Yes, in this country where we are so insecure about things like health care and basic insurance needs, it's a big thing. I know families, though, who make the decision together. They know that the breadwinner does not have his or her work, but only a job, and they know this is draining the soul of everybody, so they band together and they say, Well, let's lower our standard of living, consciously, so the breadwinner can quit and go find work. What happens in this process is that the family coheres much more closely, and community happens because they are involved together in a strategy and a commitment to the quality of life, as distinguished from just the quantity of income and consumer goods that our culture lays upon us.

MICHAEL: In some sense, your own job or work was redefined for you recently. Can you give us an update on your continuing saga relative to the Catholic Church, and describe your new job, your new work?

For years I fought to stay in my work, and the model I used was Rosa Parks on the bus. I figured she wouldn't have changed anything if she had volunteered to leave the bus, so I was not volunteering to leave the Roman Catholic Church. I think there is a great wealth there of spiritual treasures, especially from the Middle Ages, that I was helping to unearth, along with many others. And, why leave? But finally, you're right, they did give me a pink slip, and it's really quite funny, because I was in the middle of writing this book, *The Reinvention of Work.* It was a Monday morning, I was at the computer, the doorbell rang, and there was FedEx with my pink slip: 34 years as a Dominican and 26 as a priest.

So I meditated on that and said, Well, what is this? And the word that came to me was *post-denominational.* I thought, *Well, they've made me a post-denominational priest because the Catholic Church does not take priesthood away; they just, as you pointed out, don't let you practice it.* Here I was a post-denominational priest in a post-denominational time, because I think part of post-modernism is not taking boundaries too seriously, too literally. Frankly, most people today have forgotten the difference between a Lutheran and a Presbyterian and a Methodist and an Anglican and a Roman Catholic. The real issues are so big today, which are survival issues and issues about nature and creation and ecology and despair of the young, that these minor aberrations and differences that have hung around for 400 or 500 years just aren't with us anymore.

So at that time, too, I had just finished the book. The last chapter is on ritual, which surprised me because I had not had it in my outline or anything, but the idea is that the work of our time is going to be to heal human wounds, and the ritual is a big part of that. Lo and behold, two weeks after handing the book in, there appeared at my doorstep, four people from Sheffield, England— young people in their 20s. They told me the story of how they had been a community for 15 years and that in the last few years they'd been reinventing the liturgy of the Western church, the Anglican mass, using rave dancing, rap, and a lot of multimedia. And the result was such that they had 500 to 600 people at their mass Sunday nights in Sheffield, England. The average age was 27.

I was very moved by this, having just written about the importance of renewing ritual. I flew over there in November and checked it out, and I was deeply moved by the community and by the experience of the mass. To make a long story short, then I went to Bishop Swing, the Episcopal bishop here in California, and told him about it. He was very supportive. He said the church is reaching the 50- to 60-year-olds, but not doing anything for the 20-year-olds. We should just get out of the way and let them do what they need to do. So we brought over 35 of these young people to put on the mass at Grace Cathedral for two nights in a row.

What we want to do is start a community here in America, here in San Francisco, and we hope that this will be a regular thing that we'll have going. Not just the mass on Sundays, but a ritual center where we can be doing other rituals during the week. Ecumenical ones, rites of passage, and so forth. They will be recruiting the community from the rave culture and from the streets. That's how they've done it successfully in Sheffield. I think it's a real sign of hope that young people are going to be leading us into post-modern forms of worship that are much more interesting than sitting in a pew and being read at or preached at or reading books. This is about participation, it's about the body, it's about galaxies and atoms and the planets. You can reinvite into worship as our ancestors had it, through the multimedia, through the gift of technology.

MICHAEL: To me, it brings up the roots of religion, since any religion is based on the experience of the Divine, and the religion is formed around that experience. The experience is at the root. In the last quarter century, we've seen many, many Americans— young people, especially—going to religions, particularly of the East, where the experience is emphasized. So here you are pointing out that Christians in England, young Christians, are finding a way to get at that experience. It seems to me that's what's wrong, or what's happened to the Catholic Church. The experience has gone out of the church.

Absolutely. That word *experience* is so important. As Jung said, "There's a big difference between experience and belief." And belief so often goes right into our heads. And experience is that which really affects us, moves us, heals us, awakens us. If you will, it touches all the chakras. In Descartes, you find that the soul is the pineal gland. Well, that is right up on the top of your head. It just ignores the other experiences, of our emotions, of our feelings, of our body. So all my work has really been in spirituality for that reason. Because I felt that experience was the key. What did the Psalmists say? "Taste and see that God is good." You've got to taste. It's an experience.

The institution of religion can so often fall into its sociological structures, and then it becomes a thing in itself. That's where religion and spirituality split. When religion is healthy, it is a servant to spirituality, to experience. When religion is unhealthy, it draws attention to itself. It becomes kind of a sociological ego. Spirituality, then, has to be found elsewhere. As you say, many young people have sought it in the East, also in drugs. That's part of the philosophy of this group from Sheffield. These people who are doing this work and creating this community are blue-collar people, for the most part. Sheffield has a lot of unemployment, almost 25 percent unemployment. They come from damaged homes and family abuse and drug abuse and alcoholism and relationship abuse. They are healing themselves because they have such significant nontrivial work to do in terms of putting on the worship, and they are creating this community, which is also an alternative to a capitalist culture.

I think the alternative to capitalism is not communism—it's community—and I think we are ready for that now. It's just amazing what these people can do as a community. For example, some will work outside jobs, while others are free full-time to work on the ritual, and then they shift roles. They are redemonstrating the power of joint economics. They don't live under one roof. They've learned the lessons in the need for privacy, but they live in common neighborhoods, and they have this common work. And that's what makes community—the shared work.

MICHAEL: You mention unemployment. It's a universal problem, certainly, in urban areas, and even internationally as well. One of the stories you presented, which I was really impressed with in the book Reinvention of Work, *was the story of one of the Institute of Culture and Creation Spirituality's gradu-*

ates, Sister Imelda Smith, in Ireland. She went back to a commu-
nity that had 80 percent unemployment. It's a very inspiring story.

She went back as one of our graduates and went to Tala, which
is a suburb of Dublin, where as you say, there is 80 percent unemployment, and you can imagine all the abuse there, such as drug
abuse, alcohol abuse. She worked with the women first, and they
got an abandoned mansion in the area that they turned into
a women's center. Then she started teaching the women what
we call "Art as Meditation," which involves dealing with your
images, your pain, your potential for joy and hope, through dancing, clay, drawing, poetry, storytelling, and sharing. Pretty soon
the women began to be empowered. Then the men burned down
the building because they were threatened by their wives, and so
forth. So they rebuilt it and kept going.

To make a long story short, since this has been going on for
ten years, the men eventually got in on the action, too, as well as
the young people. One woman who was a member of this community came to Tala a year ago and told this story. She said she
had three teenagers, boys. When Imelda returned to Tala, they
were all on drugs, and her husband was abusive and alcoholic, and
she was just in total despair. Then she heard Imelda talk. She said
that it was the first truth she felt she had heard in her life, so she
got very involved in this community. As a result, her sons are
healthy, they are part of the community themselves, and there is a
lot happening. It is a beautiful story of rebirth and resurrection. It
didn't come from the top down. There was very little support—
economic or otherwise—for a long time. But it came from a few
good ideas and some dedicated people.

JUSTINE TOMS: *As you were telling that story, you were
talking about how they brought clay, poetry, and art into the community, and that brings up the thought of beauty. What do you feel
beauty has to do with living our lives as human beings?*

Everything. If it weren't for beauty, where would we be? One point that Thomas Berry makes about the ecological crisis is that it's not just about healthy bodies, healthy food, healthy air, but it's about where we derive our beauty. As he says, How much poetry has been written from the moon? We need beauty. We drink it. Again, we at this moment in history can no longer take it for granted. Just like we can't take healthy air or food or bodies for granted.

Lester Brown of the World Watch Institute says we have 17 years left to bring about the ecological revolution, the environmental revolution. He says the number-one obstacle is inertia, human inertia, what we call in our culture being couch potatoes, being passive. That is so interesting because inertia is traditionally a sin of the spirit, called "acedia," in its classical form. Its about not having energy to begin new things. Thomas Aquinas writes about acedia or inertia, and he says the solution to inertia is zeal. I mean, that's the opposite of inertia. Where does zeal come from? Aquinas says that zeal comes from an intense experience of the beauty of things.

So there we are back to your question. How important is beauty? Without beauty, there would be no environmental revolution. We won't get over our inertia. This is why the environmental movement has to be spiritual as well as political, because it needs to awaken people precisely through the experience of the beauty of healthy nature. I think we Americans have a special role in this. I think the wilderness is still in our hearts here in America, whereas in Europe, it's pretty much been trampled on. We still have the John Muirs and the saints of our wilderness continuing to point out that we are connected to this beauty.

JUSTINE: You've used the word interconnected. *Tell us about that circle of interconnectedness and how important that might be. I can see a whole circle there that, without the inspiration by beauty, the depression or the inertia of standing still keeps going.*

Another way to instruct people in beauty is, of course, our creation stories. This is how native people have always taught their young people—with stories to let them know that they are here for great work, not trivial work. There's a great line in Rilke that I use in the book, where he says, "Somewhere there's an ancient enmity between the great work and our daily life." The great work is creation itself. It's the ongoing universe. That's the only work really going on. Everything else has to be connected or it's trivial. We humans cut ourselves off. We get so locked up in our machine universe, our machine work, that we miss the great work.

So, our creation story today that we are getting from science moves people to awe. If you ran the film of the universe backwards from today to its origin 14 billion years ago, realizing it all began from the same pinprick of fire, up to today, it's all interconnected! Therefore, that's part of the wonder of it. We sitting here in Berkeley are connected to one trillion galaxies away from here. We're connected by gravity. We're connected by radiation. We're connected by time and space. We have the same origin. That's very moving to people, because this is not the story of the universe we've had for a couple hundred years under Newton, where the emphasis was on separation and parts. When you can feel interconnected, isn't that the essence of community? It's about feeling a connection with others.

Realize that this connection is far beyond humans. We're connected with every leaf and tree and whale. It's part of the new creation story, but it's always been part of the mystical view of the universe. Hildegard of Bingen said in the 12th century, "Everything in the universe, everything in the world, is penetrated with connectedness, penetrated with relationship." That's very beautiful. And it's a new way for us in the West of seeing the world, but it's an ancient way of seeing the world. And of course it includes the Divine Presence, too. The Divine is penetrating all things. Do we experience it, or don't we? And if we don't, we ought to quit what we're doing and take some time off—go into the desert and see what these mystics are telling us.

MICHAEL: You mentioned that we have to have an environmentalist with spirituality. I know you espouse the idea that spirituality needs to be taken into the social and political arena as well. I'm thinking of people such as Martin Luther King and Maya Angelou and Alice Walker, of contemporary times, who are active socially and politically and have a spiritual vision as well.

Yes, this view of innerconnectivity, of spirituality and politics, is both ancient and medieval and contemporary. William Hocking, the American philosopher, said early in this century, "The prophet is the mystic in action." And of course, what the prophets do is stand up and say no to injustice and wake people up. Gandhi said he learned to say no from the West. That's the prophetic tradition of Israel that affected Jesus and the Western tradition. And so you have this wonderful tradition. I think of Dorothy Day, too, and Thomas Merton and others. When you experience beauty, you experience gratitude and reverence, which are very akin. With that, then, you have the energy and, frankly, the anger, the moral outrage, to do something because when something you cherish is threatened, that is precisely when healthy anger kicks in.

There is no political movement that I've ever known that is not appealing to anger in people. Now, there is unhealthy appeal, which is the appeal of resentment that you got in Hitler. We certainly have it in Bosnia today, where the politicians are waging the war appealing to resentments between the orthodox, the Catholics and the Muslims. That's why so much of our work today has to be on the human heart. It has to be about letting go and cleansing that resentment and turning it into healthy moral outrage at injustice. At that level, we can all agree. There is a common ground where people can struggle together for justice based on a vision, which I would call a mystical vision, of what we consider to be a healthy community and healthy living.

MICHAEL: *I think many of us are unaware of how we are conditioned by what we are exposed to, particularly in the media. You bring up Bosnia. We always hear about Bosnia and the Muslims, but we never hear about the Christian Serbs. The word* Christian *is never used as an adjective of the Serbs. It's a very subtle form of editing. It doesn't address that issue.*

Yes, that is a very good point. The media can be extremely subtle and sometimes not so subtle, and it's so all-pervasive. The media is where we get our basic information today. It is the pulpit of our time because we are also getting values from the media, consciously or unconsciously.

JUSTINE: *Michael and I have discussed the media many times. It is an environment unto itself. We think of the environment as something out there that is physical. The media is definitely surrounding us in many ways, not only in radio and television and billboards and magazines—we're surrounded in all sorts of ways.*

MICHAEL: *It is so ubiquitous. We learn not to notice it.*

Exactly. You know, I did my doctoral thesis on *Time* magazine, years ago, because I sensed that, too. You are not going to get down to a critical understanding of religion's role in culture without examining critically how the media is telling us about our religion or not telling us, by what you say it leaves out. There is an amazing book that came out called *The Age of Misinformation*, by a fellow who lives out in Virginia where they had something like 120 channels. Bill McKibben sat through nine months of watching television from all the channels he could get from satellite, and then he paired that up against 24 hours at a pond. I think it is a brilliant book, and it shows just what you say, which environment do we really want to swim in and to immerse our children in? This human-made environment of media with its values, or the environment of nature itself? Somehow we have to find a better balance than we have up to now.

JUSTINE: Matthew I'd like to go back to something you began with about leaving off, taking off of work, or the letting go. I think of the image of the trapeze person who is flying from one trapeze to another. I can feel a lot of us taking our breath in and saying, Well, how exactly does one let go when it's hard enough to keep a roof over our head and keep the bills paid for eating and health care? Some of us can't even do that. What experience can you share with us?

My experience has been that if the work is timely and truly useful and important, very often (no guarantees here), the money follows. I think we presume in our country that first we need money, and then we have had work. My experience has often been that first you do the work and the money follows. This program that I started 18 years ago in Chicago that we still work at Holy Names—it's never had endowments or anything. It just keeps going every year because the students show up. They show up, and by their tuition we keep our faculty in business. It's been a lesson for me.

If you think small, with quality, you can survive. But this whole theme of letting go, of course, is one of the big mystical themes. Do we have to remain within the definition of work that our dominant culture has been giving us for a couple hundred years? This is one of the themes in the book. That we are moving from defining work in terms of the Industrial Revolution to redefining it in terms of the environmental revolution, in terms of inner work as well, and in terms of regenerating the work worlds we have. My point is this: When you check out all the unemployment in the world today, below the border it's 60 to 80 percent, and in our inner cities it's 60 to 80 percent. It's the cause of so much of our prison building.

You know, I met a man the other day who is an architect. I said, "Oh, what are you building these days?" "Prisons," he said. "It's the only work I can get in the state of California." Now it would be much cheaper for everybody and there would be less crime if we would do this prison-prevention thing called reinventing work. And reinventing education. Obviously our educational systems aren't working for inner-city kids. Are there systems that could? Well, I propose yes. You go back to the ancient peoples, and they taught their young people through ceremony and ritual and creativity. I think, frankly, it's time to try this in our inner cities. What we have isn't working. And I think that all the studies show that our most creative young people are in the inner cities. Because it takes your wits to survive there. If we appeal to the yearning for creativity there, and create a school structure around that, we might get amazing results. And it would be a prison-prevention program.

So, part of what we have to let go of today is a whole ideology of the definition of work. Just because they are closing car factories and military bases doesn't mean that work is ended. There is so much work that needs doing. But a lot of it is not the way we've been defining work during the Industrial Revolution. It's work on the human heart. It's work on unleashing creativity. Notice what these people in Sheffield, England, did. They had no money at all. These were young people. And Sheffield, England, is on its back economically. And they just felt that religion is so boring, we have two options. Go into drugs like most of our peers are, or to try to take what we do, which is computers and rave dancing and techno music and multimedia, and see if we can do something interesting. They did that, and now they have more work than they could imagine. So it's a matter of letting go of our ideologies around work.

MICHAEL: You brought up the term acedia *from the Middle Ages. Another aspect of that term involved cynicism and pessimism. This is another aspect of our culture. And as we talk about possible solutions, I can hear those voices rising up saying, Well, you're not really being realistic. You're not really seeing the real problem. What about the cynicism that pervades our culture?*

That's part of acedia, and it comes from a lack of vision and perhaps a wounded soul. It is a pessimism. Otto Rank says, "Pessimism comes from the repression of creativity." So it's really a statement about how we cannot be creative. It's like saying, "Oh, I've seen it all before." It's a yielding to the status quo. This runs counter now to the new physics. There is a new creation story from science. We are now being told that the whole universe has been bursting with creativity from the first second, the get-go of the universe. The whole universe is bursting. Well, this certainly gives us humans permission to get creative again. And especially since we are an immensely creative species. I mean, that's our problem. We've been very creative in tearing down rainforests in a day that it took nature 10,000 years to develop, and in putting holes in the ozone that it took one billion years to develop, and in creating nuclear bombs, and so forth. We obviously are creative when it comes to shadow things. It's time to get creative about rejuvenating the way that we learn and teach our young people, the way that we celebrate, the way that we grieve, the way we heal, and the way we work. I think cynicism may just be the opposite of creativity.

MICHAEL: Both you and I lived through the '60s and were in some way inspired by what happened back then. I recall that, in California, particularly, which was going through what was then called a land boom, people were buying up second home lots and places to go because the future was going to provide a lot more leisure time. Technology was going to allow people not to have to

work as much and not have to spend as much time on the job.
There was going to be all this leisure time. And yet, in point of fact,
25 years later, there is one-third less leisure time. Today people are
working more. What about that? What has happened?

Juliet Shore, a Harvard economist, talks about working more in her book, *The Overworked American.* She says that in 1948, our parents and grandparents had more leisure time, and they got 50 percent less work done per hour than we do. If we just cut back, we would have a lot more leisure time today, and that's the real issue, she thinks. We are afraid of leisure time, so we are filling it up. The problem is not just unemployment, or even the kind of work we have, but also the issue of work addiction or overemployment and the relationship between them. If people who are overworking could cut back, do something interesting with their leisure time, then there would be work available for those who are underemployed or unemployed. She feels that this actually was a crisis in the 1920s that was not faced, and then we went into the Depression and then with the war and the explosion of work that followed that, the question was not raised again.

She thinks it's a very important economic and philosophical question to ask today: What do we do with our leisure time? And, of course, what it doesn't work for is the Sabbath. The whole Sabbath tradition in Israel is about enjoying creation every seven days, every seven hours. One-seventh of our life ought to be spent in pleasure, and we are not good at that in our culture. As you say, there is this compulsion. Shore says it this way: "We live in a squirrel cage of work to spend some more." And the only way out of it, she is convinced, is to step out of that consumer mentality with the compulsion to spend, which involves the letting-go issue. It's a mystical issue, a spiritual issue. How do we learn to let go, and what do we do instead of going shopping? There are a lot of other things to do, but we often don't honor them.

MICHAEL: The consumer culture has certainly had a great effect on our approach to work and our experience of work. One of the things in the last 20 years is filling your house up with all kinds of new gadgets. Do you have the latest gadget? Do you have the latest television with a clearer picture than the previous one? This constant promotion of getting more and more material goods—that, of course, involves having to work more to have the money to buy these material goods.

JUSTINE: I had an experience recently where I live, in Ukiah, California. My assistant, Mary Buckley, had been going to a gathering of women who get together and sing together in a chorus. Finally, I got it, and I said, "Mary, you know I haven't done any singing in a long time. Can I come?" And she said, "Oh, yes, anybody, whether you can sing or not, whether you read music, everyone is invited." In this case, it was women. I went, and we made the most beautiful music together. We were just singing in rounds, that is the same melody, sung at different times, by different ones. It produces beautiful harmonies. I thought to myself in the middle of it, how this didn't cost anything, and it was certainly a lot better than shopping. It was just creating beauty for the sheer joy. It was a senseless "act of beauty."

Music not only moves your heart and awakens you, but out of it is created communication and relationship. It's creating a kind of community where everyone is feeling good about it who is involved. It costs nothing, and that's what we could be doing— making beauty in terms of the arts in our free time. We can tell our stories that way—with music, dance, gardening, planting trees, and poetry—also creating new relationships themselves. Friendship takes time. It takes a love of beauty to get to know new friends. All this is what the mystics would call developing your Being, not just your doing. Eckhart says, "We should worry less about what we do and more about who we are." Because if you are just, your ways will be just. If you are joyful, your ways will be joyful. So, that's a good example. You would be singing and praising and expressing the joy in your heart if you'd take the time to do so, with a group like that.

JUSTINE: One thing that came out of it was a discussion about how we have become such a passive culture in enjoying music. We might be getting only 10 percent of that enjoyment of what music really is. When we actually participate in it and make these beautiful sounds together and feel the resonance in our own bodies, it is so wonderful that suddenly we want to make sure that this is brought out in our communities to our children. You take the school systems that are cutting out money for what they see as nonessential, like music and art. How can we step in and make sure that this continues to happen because of what we've been talking about today?

There is a group in New York City that did exactly what you are talking about. They fired the theater department, the music department, the painting departments of the high schools. So the artists in New York got so upset by this that they started a group of their own to volunteer to go into the schools to teach art. They went out and got the financial backing, and part of the result has been that they are much freer than they were when they were being operated by the school system. Many of them prefer it to teaching the way they used to have to do in the system. Yet now they are there because the school does welcome free labor. They are still carrying on. What you say is so true, and it's so pitiful. It says so much about our culture. We don't think that art is part of training young people. It's not part of learning our way into the universe. In fact, art is the only thing that we've ever had for expressing what moves us deeply—in terms of beauty or in terms of grief.

JUSTINE: When you say art is the only language we have for expressing what happens deep within ourselves, whether it's an experience of beauty or an experience of grief, what do you mean? Is it that when your heart is moved, it's not a mathematical equation or a syllogism that is uttered—it is a "wow," or tears that flow? Or you want to dance, you want to move, you want to shout, you want to praise. You want to give away. One of the reasons we are so anal retentive in our culture, I think, is that we are not allowing ourselves, and our own school systems do not allow, ecstasy in it. It doesn't allow wonder and joy and awe.

The same is true of our religious systems. And that's why we need new forms of education that allow the body and the heart to be amazed. Frankly, that's what we've been doing in our institute for years: "Art as Meditation." It's not about talent. Like the people said, Don't worry about whether you have talent—come and sing! If you have a larynx, you can sing. The same is true of other forms of self-expression. We've overly professionalized the art world. This has not been good for the art world, either. It's been cut off from its own spiritual roots as a result.

MICHAEL: One of the sections of your book Reinventing Work *was entitled "The Great Work and the Inner Work." What do you mean by the "great work"?*

By the great work, I mean the work of creation itself—that is, of the universe unfolding—this birth of everything that has been going on for 14 billion years. Again, that phrase came from Rilke when he says we've been cut off from the great work. We have to ask how we are connected to the great work. It can't be done really without some inner work. We have to deal with our pain and our wounds and our sorrow and our anger if we are going to see the world anew and reconnect to the mystery, to the great mystery that is birthing the universe and is intrinsic to every being in the universe.

And what about inner work?

The way to inner work is through our joy, what the mystics call the "via positiva," what moves us, which is our experience of beauty and wonder and awe. And also the "via negativa," which is the experience of the dark night of the soul, of darkness, pain, suffering, of emptiness, nothingness. Either one of those paths takes us into the inner work, and one requires the other. Life, unfortunately, is not just about unending joys or unending beauty. Beauty brings terror with it, and life brings loss with it, and so we move from the beauty into the loss. But the other way is also true. People can move from darkness and despair and cynicism into a sense of childlike wonder and awe again. This, too, is inner work.

MICHAEL: There was a great article in Rolling Stone *a couple years ago about you and your work, and you were emerging from what for me has always been a very profound experience: You were coming out of a sweat lodge. I believe it was in Scotland, and it had obviously been a deep experience for you, and others were a part of it. And the author of the article said that the only words you could say at the time were: "More joy." It kind of captures what our life is all about in finding that joy.*

Yes, I think joy is the key to life. There is a wonderful quote from Aquinas. He said in the 13th century, "Sheer joy is God's. And this demands companionship." In other words, the universe exists because of the joy of God. And we can so easily forget that with our other worries. I think joy is the key to healthy work. If I were to ask people one question about their work, it would be this: "What joy do you derive from your work?" and "What joy do others derive from your work?" And if you can't answer that, if there is really no connection between work and joy for us, then it's not work; it' a job. I'm sure you and Justine, for example, must derive a lot of joy out of your work. You've certainly hung in there for many years. But do you?

*JUSTINE: Yes. Absolutely! It really is what keeps us going. I notice as I talk about my work, how my energy level starts rising. This has to do with companionship, too. You used the word com-*panionship. *I find that I am reflected in even more joy by sharing it.*

MICHAEL: I think it also goes back to community being part of the next cycle. That's certainly part of what we're involved in here, because in doing radio work, this is a community. I think community radio is really part of the new era. Commercial media, generally, is part of the machine age, it's part of the consumer culture; it promotes the consumer culture. Here we are not trying to promote the consumer culture; we are just trying to deliver information. And hopefully a little wisdom. One of the things in your book in the section about great work and inner work was a wonderful chart that was dealing with the paradigm shift and the fact that we are in transition from one age to another age. You referred to the old age as the machine age and the new one as the green era or the sheen era. I thought that was an interesting play on words. There was one machine-era item versus a green-era item that interested me. You said that enlightenment was part of the machine era, and the ecological era was part of the green era. Let's talk about the term enlightenment. *What did you mean by saying that enlightenment was part of the machine era?*

I mean the modern era's philosophy, which was called "The Enlightenment." It was an awakening of the left brain, if you will. The left hemisphere is often identified with light. You do analysis and mathematics with the lights on. But in that great achievement of light consciousness that came from the enlightenment, we have ignored the power of the darkness. Your Goddess people today will emphasize the importance of the underworld. Snakes live underground where it is dark. Our shadow and other dark, won-derful mysteries are where we also experience wisdom and truth. So the enlightenment is only part of the picture. You might say that we need a re-experience of the en-dark-ment. Now our astronauts and others who have gone out to space have found a great dark-ness out there, and this has moved them powerfully—made mys-tics of them.

MICHAEL: Many of the astronauts talk about seeing the earth in a new way, which includes a vision of the earth from that darkness—seeing the earth as a thing of beauty.

Again, it's a balance, the dark and the light, the yin/yang, silhouetted against the cosmic darkness. I think we are shifting. Another interesting thing about light is that Einstein began this century saying, "All I want to do my whole life is study light." His whole physics is based on the speed of light, since it is real-ly a special discovery of the 20th century. And, of course, what did we do with it? We turned it into atomic bombs and nuclear bombs. But now toward the end of the century, I think we are getting a little smarter, and we're saying, Well, what else can we use this light for? Whether it's computers, multimedia. Again, I say to use it for ritual, to use it to awaken the human heart and spirit so that it becomes an instrument of advancing human evo-lution instead of playing out our worst attitudes of war and dual-istic relationships.

MICHAEL: How are we going to make a conscious choice? You are suggesting one way. I'd like to hear, if you had any way to choose it, how would it be?

To choose the direction we want to go using one value of post-modernism is fun. If it isn't fun, don't trust it. I think that's a very important value. Joy, which we talked about, and, of course, justice and compassion. Compassion isn't about feeling sorry. It's about relationships of interdependence. I find that these are all tests of the authenticity of our choices. I think that reintroducing wonder and celebration is healing. This is another test. Not only is it fun, but does it elicit wonder? I think that when curiosity ceases, everything closes down.

So when we cease learning, we are already dead. There is no wisdom without curiosity. I have found many people in my life, many in patriarchal institutions, who have ceased being curious. They are just stuck there. I have found monks who aren't even curious about God. I guess they figure they have God all locked upon a box or something. It's really scary. I find university professors who are not curious about ideas. There is no wisdom without curiosity. Aquinas says, "Folly, the opposite of wisdom, comes from a dullness of the senses." There is a lot of dullness out there. We are manufacturing boredom as a civilization. We call it education. We call it worship. We call it politics. Why is it that 30 percent of our people vote in elections? It's because this modern era is no longer interesting to the people. The machine in which we've been living just isn't interesting. We are told that our bodies are machines. We've wrung whatever interest there might be out of that way of living in the world.

MICHAEL: There are so many distractions that it is hard to keep focused. Even if you are following your vision, you are surrounded by distractions all the time.

Absolutely. We really need, all of us, some of this mystical practice of silence, which is letting go of images—not just audio images, but visual images and any images. This is where meditation plays such an important role in people's lives. I'm not sure people can survive today without it. We have to take meditation away from the professionals, the monks, and as I tell in the book, we should be training our 13- and 14-year-olds in meditation.

Because meditation is our capacity to let go of images and let go of noise and get to a centered place. If you can carry that attitude with you all day, then you can, if you will, endure all this distraction without getting deep inside you. This can be done.

MICHAEL: As you wrote toward the end of the book, "Work is sacrament." What do you mean by that?

If there is only one work, the great work of the universe going on, then, the universe itself is sacrament; it is a sacred place, and it is bestowing graces on us. Our work, if it is tapping into the great work, is tapping into this bestowal of grace. Therefore, it is graceful work, it is good work, it's beautiful. If it is not tapping into the one sacrament of the universe, then it's probably not very healthy for our souls and hearts, and it's not graceful. I've written about a theology of sacrament because I've de-anthrocentrized sacrament and also taken it away from a clerical class. It's all holy. If we are doing good work, we are bestowing blessings on one another, and it all matters.

MICHAEL: It is interesting to parse that word wholeness, *and* holy *is part of* wholeness. *So the holy work is really a whole work that is being connected to the whole. Going back to something else that was in the book that I really like was your finding of the origin of the word* job, *which goes back to an obsolete word that was spelled "jobbe," which was tracked to the 19th century, when jobs were parceled out as piecework, so a job was actually a piece, which connects it to the Machine Age. A piece, a cog in a large wheel kind of thing, or a piece of something else and not really connected.*

There was piecemeal work, and how different that is from work that is connected to a great work.

MICHAEL: *Dr. Samuel Johnson, who wrote the first dictionary in the 18th century, put his definition of* job *under "the pathetic or pitiful work."*

It's amazing and instructive to go back and find etymologies of words.

MICHAEL: *It really tells us a lot about where we are today and where we have come from and what we need to come back to, to recover our roots, recover our vision. In many ways, when we are talking about this kind of work, there is less of a gap between our life and our work. It really becomes one thing, doesn't it?*

Exactly. Life is meant to be an expression of our being, and we express this in our work and at play, and it is interesting that Native American traditions do not have a word for *work*. They have a word for *play* that they use at work and that they use in other activities of living. Our culture has made too much of a distinction between living and working, being and playing.

MICHAEL: *Two years ago, I had the opportunity to go to Bali and be in the culture for about a month. One of the things we were struck by was the Balinese capacity for integrating art and creativity and spirituality into their lives and into their work. You would see someone who might be a maître d' at a little hotel or restaurant, and later you'd see them as a dancer or a carver, or they'd be an artist or all three. The Balinese have a wonderful way of integrating their play life with their work life and their spiritual life with their work life. It is all one thing to them.*

EPILOGUE

Matthew Fox envisions a world of work where intellect, heart, and health come together to celebrate the whole person. He envisions that it is possible to reinvent work so that everyone, including the estimated one billion worldwide that are unemployed, can have fulfilling work. How satisfied we are with our work relates directly to our mental, physical, emotional, and spiritual health. Everyone wants to feel useful and to make a contribution. Finding meaning and purpose in what we do is an expression of the spirit within us. Sweeping floors can be sacred labor if we identify the task with the greater whole. Through our creative endeavors, we can feel the pressure of a mystery greater than ourselves emerging from our work.

✦ Chapter Five ✦

Integrity in Business

Carol Orsborn and Michael Toms

PROLOGUE

*T*he challenges of the future are changing the face of how we
do business in America and the world today. With corporate
downsizing, mergers, buyouts, wage freezes, the global economy,
and more, the workplace is changing before our very eyes. Work
and the workplace will never be the same. Perhaps they shouldn't
be when so many more people are working longer and enjoying it
less. But what is the way out?

Carol Orsborn has followed the path that has led her out of
the traditional "work hard and you'll get ahead" syndrome. It has
led her to a new way of being and working in the world. Orsborn
first came to national attention in 1986 with the publication of
Enough Is Enough: Exploding the Myth of Having It All—A
Handbook for Overachievers Anonymous. She was the founder
and co-owner of one of the country's most respected communica-

tions and consulting companies for 25 years. She's also the author of Inner Excellence: Spiritual Principles of Life-Driven Business *and* How Would Confucius Ask for a Raise?: 100 Enlightened Solutions to Tough Business Problems. *She is the former director of the Society for Inner Excellence.*

MICHAEL TOMS: *Carol, I'd like to go back to that time when you and your husband, Dan, were deciding that you didn't want to do your business the same way anymore. Take us back there and tell us what happened.*

CAROL ORSBORN: When you say that, the first thing that comes to my mind was this horrible moment when we walked into our office and there was a half-eaten coffee cake sitting there in the conference room. Dan and I were both into power and control, and this was our business; we didn't like the fact that somebody else had convened to eat this coffee cake, and it meant that something had spun out of control. Our worst fears were confirmed, because the staff had organized against us. They felt that we had been working them too hard, that we were autocratic, hierarchical, and the sad thing was that Dan and I thought we were inspiring them. We had no idea of the discrepancy between who we thought we were and what kind of business we thought we were operating, versus who they thought they were working for.

You used to have these morning coffee klatsches, right?

Yes, and we would say inspirational things and set goals, and we were achieving higher and higher numbers, and we thought we were all together on this. We were so out of touch with what was really going on in our company. We could have noticed that we really couldn't quite make eye contact with the receptionist when we walked in and that there was a lot of time spent at the water cooler among our staff. There were signs, but we didn't see them because our numbers were good.

Then what happened?

I took one of the senior people aside and found out the depth that this went to, and I realized that I had no resources. If I went to any of the management consulting books, they were all on how to be an SOB, and management secrets of Attila the Hun and guerrilla warfare. Even the inspiring books like *In Search of Excellence*—they all said basically the same thing, which was that the way to succeed in our society was that you set a goal and that you do whatever you can to be better than the next guy. Whatever it takes, you push through your fears and your feelings, and you get that goal. I realized we'd been operating on just theory, and that you can't do more of what didn't already work in the first place. So it pushed me off of the management motivation books and I desperately went to the bookstore and started to look at saints, mystics, and gurus to see if there was any advice there for me.

Did you find advice from the mystics and saints in the books?

Yes, very much so. The consciousness of the saints, mystics, and gurus was so disengaged from the more materialistic and goal orientation that I had grown up with. It was very mind expanding. The thing was, for me, that they often talked of success as surrender and acceptance and receptivity—the process of it. I think why my books got published and why people listened to me at all is that it got beyond the philosophical understanding. I had a business that I had to run day to day, and I had to walk back into that office after this terrible incident, and over time start to find a new way of operating. What we found—even though there was a lot of pain in the middle, and I don't want to not talk about that—was that after about a year or two of really dealing with this new material and a new way of being in the workplace, we found that we were more successful than ever, and we had not expected that.

And you actually went from 20 employees to 4, wasn't it? And you sold your house?

Yes. During that period when we decided that we couldn't do any more of this driving for the goal, we decided to run our business and our lives from the point of view of, what would it take if we put our needs and our values in the central position in our life and let things fall apart around us, with the faith that it would someday, somehow reconfigure in a healthier way around us? (I don't know where the faith came from, but somehow we had this idea that if we really let it fall apart, but kept our spirit and our faith intact, it would all work out.) And it did.

Did you have a spiritual practice to carry you through this challenge?

It was very subtle, but persistent. Back in the late '60s, I stumbled onto the *I Ching,* and something kept bringing me back to that book, day after day after day, even though I have to confess to you that for the first 10 or 15 years, I never understood a single response I was getting. At some point I realized it had been subtly reprogramming me to have an open mind and to see the Eastern philosophy of not only pushing and driving for success, but also the patience and the perseverance and the receiving, which is the balance of that.

I was one of these people who from the point of my awakening at the coffee cake incident on, I was looking for a teacher, and I hadn't realized I had my teacher next to my bedstand every day. I hadn't realized where the teaching was really coming from. It did open my mind, also. I did a lot of reading in Zen and got real involved with the 12-Step materials and saw a lot of similarities to Indian philosophy and mysticism. Most recently, I've decided to delve into my own Judeo-Christian roots. I'm going to Vanderbilt University Divinity School and pursuing my master's in theological studies, with the idea that there are a lot of people—not only myself, but many of us—who are looking for the similarities and the points of contact between both the ancient and new, and our own tradition and other traditions. There are a lot of points of contact.

You are doing seminars around the country on work, and you've certainly been a consultant to corporations, and so forth. So what are you going to do with ministerial training? How are you going to integrate those two?

I'm not training to become a minister. I'm on an academic track. Most of us, when we go into the workplace, don't get to pick only people of our own faith. It is very rare when you have a business that's all southern Baptists or all New Age people or whatever. I think you have a lot of the same problems in business as you have in the school situation because we are uncomfortable, and we don't know how to broach spiritual subjects—we don't say anything. Or if we do it, we do it awkwardly. We tell people, Well, you should do what I'm doing. You try to roll everybody into your workshop or your faith or whatever. I think what we need to do is find a way to talk to one another in the workplace about our deepest beliefs, but in a way that respects diversity instead of foisting it upon people. Even more importantly, the real first step is to start acting from your deeper beliefs and to have examined your deeper beliefs.

When you talk about deeper beliefs and speaking out about them in the workplace, many people are fearful of losing their jobs, losing their position, losing whatever amount of leverage

*they may have by telling the truth and by saying how they really
feel. What about that?*

I think it makes sense to figure out which occasion is worth
rising to. You only have so much investment in any situation, and
sometimes it's worth speaking out, and sometimes it's not. You
have compulsive truth tellers, too. The way I define spirituality is
that it has to do with an inner awareness, so that you are not fool-
ing yourself. The old beliefs I'm talking about are when we buy
into the prevailing philosophy in our culture that this is a
dog-eat-dog world, that it's me against you, that it's competitive,
that in order to succeed you have to work to the point where you
hurt yourself. Those kinds of things are the unconsciously held
beliefs that really pretty much dictate how many of us behave in
the workplace.

At the level that I'm writing and teaching, it's very much
focused on the individual at this point. It's saying, Take a look and
see to what degree those things are expressing themselves in your
life. If you are a workaholic, I promise you that those kinds of
reward-and-punishment fear-driven derivatives are part of what is
going on for you. A person who has an actively practiced spirituality in which they feel that the universe truly wants them to succeed, and is truly loving, will not think that they have to damage
themselves in order to be successful.

*Do you find that you are working less time now and that you
have more quality time, or are you working more and enjoying it
more because you are more integrated with your work?*

I've done both. At the first stages of recovery, I had to work
less because I needed to have long blocks of time to take long
walks in nature and journal and meditate. I had to remember what
it was like to hear my inner voice. My inner voice whispers. My
external life shouts.

It's a good metaphor.

It takes some stepping outside. I'm pretty in tune with my inner voice after many years now of taking the time to listen. What I really advise people to do, and what I do, is to work appropriately. Work with passion and inspiration, and recognize when it's turning from the joy and the inspiration into being driven by fear. Watch for when that moment happens, and deal with it, and don't just go into automatic overdrive with the adrenaline taking over the wheel.

The subtitle to the book How Would Confucius Ask for a Raise? *is* 100 Enlightened Solutions for Tough Business Problems. *Now, the solutions that you've given here are based on your experience of the* I Ching. *I'm wondering how you came up with the questions. Where do the questions come from?*

Over the last four or five years, I've been doing a lot of traveling around the country, going to business groups, whether it's Prudential Insurance or Apple Computers, whatever, and at the end there would always be people who would say, "Your philosophy sounds great, but what do I do in my situation...I'm about to get fired, or the IRS is auditing me, or the secretary is the boss's niece." Something like that. I really believed that my philosophy would work on a day-to-day basis in a real practical everyday kind of sense. I started keeping notes of the toughest challenges, with the idea that if I thought about it long enough and really took some time out to apply my philosophy in a practical way, it would indeed give the kind of guidance and advice that people are looking for.

You found that your philosophy did indeed answer at least 100 problems.

I didn't dodge any tough questions. I thought of the 100 toughest ones I really could, and the thing is that every once in a while, the book spins off into prayer or meditation or acceptance or even humor because there's a lot of situations that aren't going to resolve the way you want them to. The gift of the *I Ching* and Confucius has to do with accepting that life is conditioned and unfree. I grew up in San Francisco in the '80s. I grew into adulthood in the '80s and '90s where so many of the workshops and philosophies were saying that you can have it all, you can have it your way, basically you can have control over everything. At first it was if you work hard enough, if you're smart enough, if you try hard enough, and then it got to be, if you meditate enough, if you eat enough healthy food. But a lot of it was still about control issues. And so one of the things that I've been working on in my life, and one of the things that I'm trying to teach to people—particularly in business—is, how you can operate in situations where you don't necessarily have control and to understand that you are not always going to be able to have control.

Why do you think it's so difficult for most of us to give up wanting to control? We always want to make sure it's safe or secure or that we can control it. Why is that?

I think the serious answer is just that our institutions—our religious and spiritual institutions—aren't really functioning well for us in this day and age. We've got the backlash from the Age of Enlightenment. There was a time when people did have faith in things. Not that it was always going to work out in this lifetime, but there was a sense that there was an ultimate fairness. And when the enlightenment came in and the Age of Reason, a lot of people started to question whether this really was a loving universe. If you couldn't test it out scientifically, did it exist? Was it real? So in contemporary society, we have the backlash of that, and we have a lot of people who've had their own faith structures

taken away, and I believe that they are going to come back anyway, because things like the new science are bringing us full circle back into the mystery, which is where we need to be.

In the meantime, we did have this illusion that if you were
uncomfortable you could use the scientific method to decrease
your comfort. So you didn't need faith. You could go out and
invent electric heating or the electric lightbulb or something. You
didn't need faith. You could get it by using your rational mind, so
it gave us this illusion of being powerful.

*It's interesting that in some ways Einstein discovered the theory
of relativity in 1915, but now 75 years later, many of us and many of
our institutions are still living a pre-Einstein view of the world.*

Einstein asked a very inspirational question. He said that the
one question that every human being has to ask of him or herself
is, "Is this a friendly universe?" That is the ultimate question.

Do you think it's friendly?

I'm banking on it.

What's your experience?

My experience is that things that at the time feel uncomfortable or are really, really difficult have had hidden gifts in terms of
the growth and development of my character and my spirit. I've
come to believe that the old paradigm, which was that you push
through your feelings, your fears, your character, and your spirit in
order to get the result—that's how you define success. In the new
paradigm, I think many of us are beginning to understand that the
greatest success comes out of the growth and development of your
character and your spirit. If, because of the hard knocks, you
become a more compassionate person or you have more humility

or more open-mindedness, and there is some sort of ultimate orderliness that is beyond my human comprehension, then I need that thought to get through the day, because if all we're doing is going toward chaos, then I think that it would be challenging to want to continue to contribute.

Joseph Campbell used to say, in looking back on his life—and he was using it as an analogy for others' lives—that you see events that occurred that may appear at the time as tragedies or real disasters, but with the passage of time and the passage of other events, you look back on them and you realize it was a real turning point—it was a time of a crossroads, perhaps, or a shift in direction. The turning points seem to be kind of cosmically ordained, heaven sent, even though at the time we were experiencing them, they were not that experience at all. It goes back to the I Ching—*perseverance furthers the ability to hang out in the unknown and brings us to a place of understanding and resolution.*

I think there's an essential shift that happened in consciousness that hasn't really served us well, which is to the degree that spirituality has been equated with only being comfortable or being joyful or happy. I think that's done us a real disservice, because if you go back to the Old Testament and look at a lot of images of faith, you see that faith is really demanding. I mean, to truly have faith in the universe is not about putting on a superficial happy, smiley face and everybody being nice to each other.

To bring it back to business imagery, I know that some people think that spirituality in the workplace means that if you are going to be a spiritual person in the workplace, you're nice to everybody all the time. I'm much more in the kind of faith and spirituality that forces you to struggle with the real issues about when do I take a stand? How can I balance my need to make a living with giving expression to my values? I think there are a lot of places where a lot of people who could be a lot happier in their jobs in the world have gotten into trouble by thinking that their jobs should do it all for them, that their jobs should be the simple, wonderful place where everything works out all the time.

Isn't that true about most things we do? We externalize our deliverance in some way? We see our deliverance as outside of ourselves, either with our work or with a teacher or with a lover or whatever and whoever it might be. It's external to ourselves. We really have to bring it home, don't we?

Yes, and in the workplace you have the Peter Pans that are jumping from job to job looking for the job that's going to give them everything, instead of taking a look at what their needs are. In the book *How Would Confucius Ask for a Raise?*, I tell the story about a poet—she is actually a friend of mine—who lives in San Francisco. She works for the government and had for many years, and decided to take this huge leap of faith because she read a book that said that if you follow your heart, your dreams will come true. And so she left her secure position and took some time out to write this wonderful book of poems and then circulated it around to about 20 editors, and at the end of this period of time found out that nobody wanted to publish her book. So she went to sit down with an aunt of hers who's very wise, and she said, "Aunt, where did I go wrong? I followed my heart. I took the risk. I put my life on the line. Why didn't it all happen for me?" And her aunt turned to her and said, "Well, you know, dear, it works a lot better if when you look into your heart, there's an investment banker inside."

We've lost this concept of heroism in our society the idea that when you find your passion, your purpose, it might not be something that also brings you money and comfort and social status and prestige. Those of us who were writing books about spirituality and business ten years ago can really see that that's true.

I'm fond of saying that in Marsha Sinetar's bestseller, Do
What You Love, the Money Will Follow, *she didn't say how much.
Because so often when you do follow your heart, it doesn't necessarily lead to lots of money, but it can lead to lots of satisfaction
and different kinds of values, different kinds of rewards.*

My experience overall has been that the more I surrender, the
more money I make and the less I need it, so I'm really at a point
now where I make my decisions based on following my heart, figuring out what my purpose and passion is. But I'm not averse to
doing a job for money, either, as long as it's not destructive to the
environment. I'll take on a project that is maybe less than fulfilling my potential in order to make some money. There was a time
in my life where I felt that everything had to be like the outer
edges of my expression of myself and hold the promise of having
it all. I think that most lives work better if you can separate out
what your purpose and passion is from where you have to make
your income.

If the two come together, great; it happens for some people
sometimes, but there are many people who are working 70- or
80-hour weeks at a job that kind of looks like it should lead them
to where they are going. I'm thinking of all the people in public
relations or advertising who really are meant to be writers or
poets. There are a lot of these fields that look close enough, such
as jingle writers who really want to be songwriters. There are so
many fields that look like a compromise, but if only I get good
enough at it or do it smart enough, my whole life will come
together around it. Those tend to be the glamour jobs that take
working in the media 70 or 80 hours a week. They are crazy
schedules; they are never going to be anything other than that. So
there are a whole lot of people who are leaving the so-called
glamour field and taking jobs, say, selling in bookstores or things
like that, and then they can go home at five o'clock. They don't
have to stay there till midnight. What they can do at five o'clock

is they can write or serve the community in some way to find some expression for their true purpose that was never going to be satisfied on the track that they were on.

Those who have more time can spend some time with their children and their families.

I have two children; one is 16. I better get used to the idea that he's getting up there. I started my writing ten years ago, and it's not accidental that my youngest is ten. I was right at that particular point where I realized—wait a second—I have this image of being successful, of having the house and romping with the kids on the green lawns. In order to afford this dream house that we had at that particular point, I was going to have to be at the office all the time, and it was going to be the nanny who was going to be romping on the lawn with my kids. I'm glad I made those changes back then.

It's like birthing a baby and then having to birth yourself.

That's exactly what happened. It was pretty much simultaneous.

In your book Inner Excellence, *you enumerated seven principles of life and business. Do those principles still hold true for you?*

Yes. I have to say that what happened to me between *Enough Is Enough*, my first book, and *Inner Excellence* is that I wanted to think about some principles that were big enough that would encompass the rest of my life, and I think I managed to do that. Because I kind of outgrew *Enough Is Enough* since it said that if you have to choose between success and values, choose values. And that was back in the mid-'80s when it was very important that we hear the message about downward mobility as being an all-right option, and you can't have it all, and things like that. And I really did think it was about choosing. So it made a lot of sense for me to cut the size of my business back, move from the big house to a small house, pull the kids out of private school, all that kind of stuff, because those things all represented a use of my time and my resources in a way that didn't reflect my values.

I found that I needed a lot less than I thought I needed as long as I was spending my time on the right things. But as I said before, what happened was, the more time I spent taking care of myself, the better things did around me, and so, with *Inner Excellence*, I realized that I was going to have to somehow expand my thinking to incorporate the fact that there was no discrepancy between taking care of myself and my success. In fact, there seemed to be a positive correlation. And that's where the principles of *Inner Excellence* came from—trying to figure out how surrender and acceptance can actually make me more successful.

What are those principles from Inner Excellence*?*

The first principle is: Change your beliefs about the nature of business and life, and you will change how you manage your career. If you think of this as a dog-eat-dog world, then you are either going to be a dog, or you're going to eat a dog. Joseph Campbell said that our beliefs are like software programming, and if you change the programming, you'll change how you act in the workplace. If you come into the workplace with the expectation that everything that happens to you is a gift, you are not going to have the same fear-driven responses that most people have. If you think it's a dog-eat-dog world, of course, nobody wants to be eaten by a dog! And fear does not provide stability. You become reactive. You become withdrawn—the whole concept of reactivity as opposed to being truly creative.

In some ways, it closes off your channels, too. It closes off your receptors. You can't receive anymore when you close down with fear.

Yes. Most people start their careers out of inspiration, and at some point it shifts into fear, and you'll know when you've shifted into fear when you say things to yourself like, "Well, if I don't do X, I'm going to fall behind," or "The boss will see me." Those are fear responses. This is the water most of us swim in, so we don't even realize how much of our ambition is driven by fear.

When we say, "My desk isn't clean, I have to spend more time cleaning my desk," it's really fear motivated, isn't it?

You might be inspired to clean out your desk. If you want your desk clean because it will give you the ability to be more creative and to be more inspired, that's fine. But if it's because, the boss might walk in the room and see it or you're going to lose things, I don't know.

The second principle is: In order to become fully successful, you must first be fully alive. That to me has to do with the fact that so many people only want to live in the comfort zone. A very wise woman said to me, "You know, the point of life is not to expand your comfort level; it's to expand your discomfort level."

The third principle is: When you empty yourself of the illusions of who and what you think you are, there is less to lose than you had feared. A lot of people are scared to death of being discovered or exposing the truth of who and what they are. For instance, I talked about the coffee cake scene earlier. I was the cheerleader for the staff coming in and being hyper, trying to get the whole staff motivated and all that, because on some level I was afraid that they didn't respect me. The truth is that they really didn't respect me, so I might as well find out what the truth is. What am I really dealing with here?

I think there are a lot of people in positions of power—CEOs, managers—who are really scared to death of being found out and, in fact, have gone to hide in their positions of power. We were talking earlier about the workplace needing a transformation, and I would say that one of the key things I think would help our work-places be more vital would be if power weren't held arbitrarily. Right now, if there is power that's being held arbitrarily in a company, the person who is holding it arbitrarily knows and can feel it in their unconscious, if not their conscious, so that they don't really have a firm grip on the place. They don't really have the loyalty of the troops. The people really don't buy into their vision. Meanwhile, the people who are working for somebody who has arbitrarily held power don't respect that person.

Companies can go on for years pretending that none of this is true. For example, the boss comes in and says inspirational things, the staff hustles to anticipate the boss's needs because they are afraid of being fired, and the thing seems to be operating well enough, but eventually, it catches up with the company. I think this is a lot of what's happening with these mega-corporations that are having financial problems right now—big turnover problems, huge disability payments, stress-related disability issues, losing top CEOs and middle-manager people who will leave with the business.

The next principle is: You have the choice between being the victim of circumstances and being empowered through them. That's what we were talking about before, similar to what Joseph Campbell again said: "It works better if you take life as if it were a gift," as if it were meant to be of your own choosing, even when it's not. For me is, it really has to do with holding consciousness on two tiers simultaneously. On the one hand, knowing and admitting my powerlessness and putting the overall destiny of my career, my business, my life, in the hands of a Higher Power, while simultaneously being willing to take everything as if it were my own doing. I think it's the holding both things at once that seems contradictory, but really does work well together.

The next principle—it may be my favorite—is: When you are driven by life, the odds will be with you. I only found this out through experimentation. I began to notice that there was a direct correlation to when I could get outside of fear as the motivating factor and start to be inspired and enthusiastic. Enthusiastic means to be filled with God. I noticed that things tended to work better for me sooner or later. Not always when I custom-ordered them, but sometimes it would almost be instantaneously. Sometimes I would have a breakthrough, and I would realize, no, I'm not in control and I surrender and I have faith, and then the thing would manifest almost immediately. I began to notice that when you are driven by life, the odds will be with you. I thought a long time about this particular principle because I didn't want to put guarantees on there, so I really see it as odds, and that takes into consideration our human limitations.

What about risk taking relative to that one?

The thing about risk taking is that a lot of people only want to take a risk when they know it's going to turn out for themselves, which means it's not a risk. A lot of people say, Well, I'd take the risk if I knew it was going to work out.

When you use the term life-driven *in the risk-taking activities of whatever kind, whether they be risk taking in business or risk taking in running a river, or whatever it happens to be, they tend to be very life-enhancing activities, in the sense of, you really realize you are alive. They remind you that you are alive.*

Somehow I've made the move from being a person who's working 80- or 90-hour weeks at a business in which I was pretty deadened and burned out, stressful, feeling alienated from myself and the world—somehow I managed to go from there to where I am now—working full time as a writer and speaker and pursuing my master's. I'm having a good time now, and people say, Well, you must be lucky. My real gift is a gift that's available to everybody, which is to be willing to walk off the edges of cliffs (into the void) when you aren't happy. I've done it, I guess, three or four times since 1986: First, when we cut the size of our business back. Then I decided to leave the business and work full time as a writer when there was no external reason in the world to think that I could make a living doing it. Then we moved to Nashville, which was a big move from San Francisco, leaving everything behind to pursue our dreams.

The list goes on and on, but I am one of those people who has gone through the dark night of leaving behind the status quo and the comfort and going through that sense of, will it ever come back together for me again? I've noticed that my husband's and my comfort levels have really increased by the fact that we've let things fall apart beneath us and have come out okay. I see other people hanging on, and all that happens is that they are hanging on to something that doesn't work, and it still doesn't work.

Both you and your husband were partners in your business, right?

Right. What's happened is that Dan really, really wanted to work in the music business, which is why we moved to Nashville. He loves country music; he loves writing. Recently he landed this position with Warner Brothers records as his client, and he's involved in a writers' community. The wonderful thing about Nashville is they've got this model of creativity that is just ideal for the whole world. I wish the whole world could have this kind of collaborative co-writing experience that is sort of reminiscent of Paris in the '20s. These are artists and musicians who are mostly struggling—they don't have a whole lot of money, but what they have is this great joy of working together to capture emotions in music. They really are pulling each other up. It's really a wonderful thing—what I'm seeing in Nashville—that I haven't seen anyplace else.

It sounds like something similar that emerged in San Francisco in the '70s, called the Briarpatch Network a network of small businesses, enterprises, and people having to subscribe to principles of sharing expertise with one another and ideas and thoughts and brainstorming. Even sharing open books, finances, and so forth.

I think we so crave community. I think that going through the individualistic self-improvement outside of institutional religions and spirituality was an important phase for many of us to go through, because in order to break out of being part of an institution that is dysfunctional, you have to spend some time with yourself alone. But I think that there are a lot of us who are ready to come back and play in community and who want to find each other and to now try and put into practice what they've been finding as individuals. I think that's the next step. Many people come to me privately after a talk and say something like, Well, I really practice these spiritual principles in my own life, but it's scary to bring it into the workplace because that's where my livelihood is. That's where the survival issues are. If only all those people would take the risk of being more fully and wholly themselves—not only in the workplace but in their lives. To take those kinds of risks. To say, I matter and I don't have to blindly follow anybody else's ideas about how this has to be; I can be a leader. That's the kind of grass-roots spirit that is welling up right now.

We don't need single leaders anymore. What we need are plural leaders, or many people leading.

I'd like to define leadership, because this was another great gift from the *I Ching,* the ancient Chinese philosophy. The *I Ching* says that what's really important is that you find out what your appropriate level for participation is in any given adventure. Sometimes you may find that you have the ability to be the leader, the center that has legitimate power, not arbitrary power. And people will spontaneously want to gather around you and support you. But there are other times when you may have a desire to see something happen, and you realize you don't have the leadership qualities, and then it's just fine to become a supporter of somebody else who you do respect. I think this is the piece that most contemporary businesses in our contemporary work environment really lack. We don't honor those people who are going to be great support people, and nobody gives themselves permission to ask the question: Is the way that I'm going to express my leadership to be a great support person to somebody else?

I think of a baseball team as a community—players coming together around a common cause. Not any one of them is really the leader, as such. One of them gets appointed captain, and it's a great honor because of the realization that this is a team, and no one person is really the leader. But one person gets elected a captain. It's that kind of community that I think we need more of, if I can use the baseball metaphor for a moment. I think the challenge of the '90s and into the 21st century is really coming back to community in a much larger way.

I don't know enough about baseball to know the role of the captain, but what if the captain tends to be someone who epitomizes the qualities of what they are looking for?

The captain would epitomize the qualities of a leader, of someone who everyone on the team would want to emulate.

It's not necessarily the person who has the best skills; it's more than that. Our business got a lot stronger when we realized that we shouldn't always hire the person who has the highest and best skills. That it's really the whole character—the whole person and who they are. The integrity of them really makes the difference.

Here we have two more principles of Inner Excellence *to cover. What are the last two?*

The sixth principle is: Your ordinary self is enough. That is giving permission for people who felt that they were going to have to be something other than who they naturally are to be successful. And who therefore ignore or squash down their inner voice, their personal needs, in order to be successful.

The seventh principle is closely related, and that is: To achieve greatness, you must be willing to surrender ambition. You see, what tends to be true about truly great people, when you read their biographies, is that they are people who have a real strong mission or purpose, and they are in touch with their inner imperative, so they are always doing what's next. Just do what's next. That's the key to achieving greatness in your career and in your business and in your life.

Yes, and also not getting caught up in the whole fame thing.

Some people are so focused on the goal; it's as if they throw the goal ahead as an anchor, and then they pull themselves toward it, and the only time they are going to give themselves any kind of stroke or validity is when they reach that goal. So the process doesn't contain any of the richness or the gifts. It's seen as the stuff that they have to do before they get to the goal. And lo and behold, what happens when they get that goal is that they maybe spend ten minutes celebrating, and then they have to set the next goal, so they don't get very much joy in their lives.

It's an empty reward. What about people who don't have jobs? People who are not working, and people also who don't have companies? They are wage earners. First, what about people out of work?

There are so many people who are either out of work or who realize that the structures that they are in aren't going to sustain them for the long term. We used to think that our jobs were going to take care of us for our whole lives and that we could invest our loyalty in them, and that they would, therefore, take care of us. People who follow the principles that we were talking about in *Inner Excellence* have the best chance of succeeding into the '90s because they are developing a sense of the fact that their success is going to be held inwardly. Being unemployed or having challenges in the workplace that are insurmountable does not mean that they have failed in any way. There isn't any of this sense of, gosh, everybody else is having it all. I did something wrong. I'm bad. Or whatever. You see, I think this idea that you can have it all, and if only you are a good enough person you will have exactly what you want, has had this sort of backlash to it. A lot of people feel that they have failed personally.

What is going on is that our systems are failing. It is the system. It is the institution that is failing. Actually, the truth is that when you pick up the newspaper every morning and find out that 2,000 have been laid off here, 10,000 here, you do start to get the feeling that there are some major shifts going on. One of the questions in the book that a lot of job seekers say to me is, "I've become depressed by the job-hunting process. How am I ever going to get my next job?" And I'll say to them, "That's one of those things from the '80s or '90s that said you needed a positive attitude to get a job. The truth is that you can have a positive attitude, and it can take longer than you think to get the job. And you can also have a negative attitude, and as long as you keep your résumé going out there, you may get the job." We are not in control. I think that is the ultimate issue for me. Where my spirituality comes into play is to understand the serious demands that mature spirituality makes upon us. That faith makes demands, and it is a struggle because it isn't about having control. It's about having faith.

It's about commitment and intention, too, I would imagine.

Absolutely. I don't think that you can really have commitment or intention unless you have faith, unless it's being fueled by fear, in which case, sooner or later something's going to spin out of your control. And that's when you get these superstars—people who do great in their companies until the first major glitch comes, and they don't have the resources to back it up when something goes wrong. I feel sorry for people who have meteoric rises to power, because when something does go wrong, and it may not even be in the workplace (it may be a marriage that fails or a drinking problem or a health problem), these are the people who really hit bottom. They get into their 50s or 60s, and they had a meteoric rise, they understood how to play the power games, and they have no resources.

I look at all these people, like the people who are out of work now, the people who have had their lumps and their bumps, and I'm definitely in that category. Some of it was self-chosen, but some of it has definitely been imposed. I realize that I've had to develop the kind of resiliency that could handle failure and setbacks and not let it take me under. As we go into the '90s and into the new millennium, we can't trust the systems to take care of us for life. Those of us who have had our lumps and bumps are really going to be best suited for being successful in the future.

EPILOGUE

Carol Orsborn makes us an offer that's hard to refuse. We can work less and achieve more. She comes from her own direct experience of choosing to cut her work hours and suffer what she thought would be the inevitable consequence: fewer financial and professional rewards. Much to her surprise, she didn't have to give up either; in fact, she increased both. The free time she gained by working less allowed her to think more clearly and more effectively. Her work was now fueled by inspiration, creativity, and desire—not by fear, resentment, and deadlines. The quality of the work increased as did the quality of life. What happened for Carol is available to each of us as well. The choice is ours to make.

✦ CHAPTER SIX ✦

The Soul of Business

Dr. Keshavan Nair and Michael Toms

PROLOGUE

Perhaps as a response to the greed decade of the '80s, a new and emerging movement is gathering momentum in the midst of one of America's most entrenched institutions: business, the corporate environment. There are those trying to bring a new ethic to the world of business doing business as if people and the planet mattered. This is not a blue sky, head-in-the-sand ideal, but rather a serious and committed effort to literally transform the way business is conducted.

One of those at the forefront of this trend is Dr. Keshavan Nair, with over 30 years' experience as a corporate executive and management consultant. As a life-long student of the teachings and life of Gandhi, he provides counsel to large Fortune 100 companies as well as small emerging companies on leadership development and strategic decision making. He is the author of

Beyond Winning: The Handbook for the Leadership Revolution *and* A Higher Standard of Leadership: Lessons from the life of Gandhi.

MICHAEL TOMS: *I am interested in when you first became exposed to Gandhi and how that was for you.*

KESHAVAN NAIR: Like most young Indians of my generation, we were great admirers of Gandhi, but thought he was sort of impractical. It was only at a certain point in my life, when I fell ill and I had plenty of time to read, that I started studying his life and became convinced that my view of him had been superficial. I had focused, like many people do, on his ascetic lifestyle, on his clothing, and all those sorts of things. What I realized was that his real qualities were related to courage, commitment to ideals, and high principles, and all the rest of it was a way of reinforcing these for him and for the people he was trying to lead. The essence of him was really stating his ideals publicly and having the courage and the commitment to try to live up to them. I began to realize that to publicly say, "Here are my ideals," and then spending his entire life trying to live up to them represented a heroic life. I realized that Gandhi was a true hero, and that's how I began to try to get an appreciation for who he was in a more practical sense.

The word commitment *really implies something beyond just doing something or just acting in a certain way. It means you're going to do something no matter what you've come up against.*

That is the essence of having an ideal. Gandhi always felt that ideals were essential for inspiring the human spirit because they put our potential before us. He recognized that ideals, by definition, are not attainable. What is essential is commitment—and to do our best to live up to them in all circumstances that come before us. He was the first to acknowledge and demonstrate by his own life that he couldn't live up to those ideals all the time. But the idea of commitment to them was essential so that you knew when you were wrong.

Now I believe that ideals can be viewed in two ways. Unfortunately, most of us look at our ideals and see how far we are from them and get depressed. But you can look at it another way. Your ideals and where you are—the difference is the potential that you have compared to where you want to go. It's not a depressing thing; it is potential. Because in this kind of quest, you can think of yourself as having equal potential to everybody else. There is nobody gifted in this kind of activity. It's not like athletics. You don't have to be tall, you do not have to be physically strong. This is a quest and a commitment of spirit. Everybody has within them those same qualities of spirit. So Gandhi often said, and he believed, and though I'm not sure everybody else would, that anybody could have done what he had done. He claimed it was nothing extraordinary, and he had no special divine mandate or special gifts. This was all self-study and self-commitment. And that is what I think he teaches. To take personal responsibility for your own life, lead it yourself, and live up to your ideals.

If you take that principle and apply it to the organization or, say, to business, then we're talking about the difference between someone who's working in an organization who's really committed to the ideals of the business or the product of the business or the service of the business, versus somebody who's basically just filling in time and doing what has to be done and then going home, and that's it.

That's a really good point, because when I talk of his true principles, his fundamental principles, which were truth and nonviolence, I said to myself, "Now wait a minute, how does this apply to business?" Well, when you think about it a little bit, it becomes obvious. If you believe in truth, how can you do any false advertising? If you believe in truth, how can you do anything but create the best product or provide the best service for your customers? If you believe in truth, how can you not believe in total quality? All these things become fundamental to the way you do things. They don't become the latest management fad, because if you are truthful, all these things are automatic. Now if you think of violence, people think of physical violence. But to Gandhi, violence meant any form of oppression or discrimination. Poverty, he thought, was a form of violence. So if you believe in nonviolence, how can you discriminate against minorities, how can you discriminate based on gender? How can you stab somebody in the back to get ahead?

When you put these together, you begin to realize that a lot of these so-called management theories that we espouse should be based on fundamental ideals. For example, one of the things we learn is that the reason that businesses get into trouble so often is that they don't see reality. The U.S. auto industry didn't see the reality of Japanese competition. Part of the problem is, people have the data, but they don't want to see it. It is one of the essential tasks of senior management to acknowledge the current reality. Now if you are committed to truth, then your commitment to acknowledge reality becomes much stronger. You try very hard because you're committed to truthfulness.

So these two principles are not some abstract things that don't have practical application. They really make you succeed. And that is the message I try to put forward: These are fundamental principles. So if you come to your business from a moral point of view, then you will not change your principles every time the bottom line changes a little bit. And that's really the essence of the argument. If you approach quality, service—all these things— from the concept of principles like truth and nonviolence, then you won't change it just because you had a little bottom-line trouble last year.

Hasn't it always been the overriding force in American business that the bottom line is what counts, and we have to do everything we can to make the bottom line. The idea has been, well, if we spend too much money on the product and make it a better product, we're not going to have as big a bottom line. What about that kind of conditioning that we have about business?

I think that's changed a lot. I think people are now realizing that quality—the thing done right the first time—is always better, and that you actually save money. It is like truth. If you are truthful the first time, then you don't get caught in the web of lies. It's the same concept. To be truthful that first time saves you a lot of heartache over subsequent events. If you have very good quality, it's the same principle. You then don't have to correct yourself. You don't have to find defective parts and correct them, which now has been proven to be very expensive. When we started out with quality, everybody said, "Oh, this will be too expensive." Now everybody knows it's cheaper (if you want to use that word) or more efficient to be truthful the first time. You don't spend your life correcting what you should have said the first time. So the underlying principle remains the same if you are trying to do the right thing.

What about on the employee level? We see companies that are downsizing and moving their manufacturing operations to Taiwan and Mexico and other Southeast Asian countries to get cheaper wages.

I think there is one essential thing we have to understand. Business is a commercial enterprise, and it will not be possible to maintain the highest ideals in business, because there are conflicts that occur. It's true beyond business, whether you are a physician or a lawyer or a broadcaster, you're not trying for sainthood. These conflicts occur when there are two principles that you subscribe to which lead you in opposite directions. For example, in the case you brought up, one principle says, I've got to keep my company afloat by staying competitive through cutting costs; the other is, I do not want to lay off anybody. It may not be possible to do both. Then you've got to ask yourself a question. These two principles are in conflict. They are both good principles. I want to keep full employment, but I want to keep my company afloat. Then the issue becomes, Which principle do you think creates the best for the most people?

But then when you've answered that question, you've got to answer the next question: How can I minimize the impact on the people that are going to be negatively impacted when I make this decision? That's why you've got to talk about severance pay, training, education, all those sorts of things.

The question of job security has a broader context as the needs of the corporation change. Recently I saw an article in the *Wall Street Journal* on a CEO of a big semiconductor company. He said something to the effect of, "Look, I cannot tell you what the future is going to be. Therefore, I can't guarantee you employment. But my responsibility is to provide you the opportunity, the training, education, courses, et cetera, so that you can prepare for any changes that might come about. That's my responsibility. Your responsibility as employees is to take advantage of that."

Gandhi stressed the idea of individual responsibility. He said that responsibilities are more important than rights. As a matter of fact, he said that rights come after meeting your responsibilities. If you don't meet your responsibilities, you have no rights. Now if we all met our responsibilities, society would be very different, because then people would not have to struggle for their rights. Now are we a society driven by rights, which creates a lot of problems for us, because a society driven by rights is a society of advocacy, confrontation, and trying to split up the pie. A society driven by responsibility is one of compromise, taking care of the needs of other people so they don't have to struggle for rights. If you think of it philosophically, you say, why did the African Americans have to struggle for their rights?

Might this not be the difference between socialism and capitalism?

Idealistic definitions of both of these work pretty well. Because in both of these cases, the underlying moral principles were always the same. Some of the people who first founded capitalism were very religious and strict about meeting their individual responsibility to their fellow man. Socialism focused on the material needs of people. The founders in this case also recognized the importance of the needs of the spirit. It's when both of these diverge from their central humanistic principles—when socialism becomes the state, and capitalism becomes purely money—that the needs of the individual are not being taken care of.

You were going to make a point about African Americans.

African Americans in this country had to struggle for their rights because the rest of us didn't meet our responsibilities to them, to treat them as we would like to be treated. If we had met that responsibility, why would they have had to struggle for their rights? That's the same with Americans for Disabilities; the same is true with gender. It's when one group fails to meet their fundamental responsibilities—that is, treat other human beings as you would like yourself to be treated. Then they have to struggle for their rights. If you met your responsibilities, then you wouldn't have this problem of others struggling for their rights. Now we still have to have the Bill of Rights to protect ourselves from people who abuse power, but fundamentally if we met our responsibilities, the rights issues would not be as contentious as they are today.

One of the things I've noticed about looking at the life of Gandhi is that he lived very simply, to the point where he dressed in a loincloth and carried a blanket around with him at times. He was someone who shied away from attachments, and this again is another interesting area when applied to business. In business you're talking about having to attach yourself to so many things.

That is one of the great challenges. To go back to Gandhi, when he started his life in politics, he asked himself a question, which went something like this: "What will help me to free myself from political corruption, as well as the possibility of temptations that arise in public life?" The first thing he recognized was that he should embrace voluntary poverty. Because if he embraced voluntary poverty, then he would not be tempted by material things. Nobody could give him any gifts, nobody could do anything for him, he had no house, he had no insurance policy, he had no bank account, he had nothing. When he died, he had, as you said, his loincloth, his sandals, an old watch someone had given him, his spectacles, and his little statues of three monkeys—that was all he possessed.

Gandhi was so committed that even when he went to see the King of England for a reception, he never changed his dress.

That's right. He wore his loincloth. He considered himself to be representing the poor of India. We talk about identification with our customer. His customer, if you think of it that way, was the poorest of the poor in India. And he never wore more than what they could afford. And so that was his representation. He identified with the people he was trying to serve and did not work for personal gain. If you have detachment, the ideal state that we refer to in all traditions is that you work for the work itself, without desire for its fruit. That is the ideal state.

This is really karma yoga.

Yes, selfless action. Work without desire for the fruit. Now the problem that we have in business is, of course, that the fruit is really the issue. You want to succeed at the profession, you want to earn more money. Now what I say is, Look, it's not practical to ask somebody in business (or, for that matter, in law, medicine, journalism, et cetera) to work without any desire for the fruit. If you were doing that, you'd be a saint, so let's eliminate that idea. Let's understand the concept that attachments can have a corrupting influence. That's the first thing, acknowledgment of the problem. What some people find it hard to understand in a consumer-driven society is that attachments can have a corrupting influence.

First, we've got to understand that at some point we've got to say to ourselves, "I have enough." For some people, that is never so. But the quicker you say you have enough, the quicker you become exempt from the pressure that we put upon you to get more. That is the second step. There are people in history who have had lots of wealth, lots of money, lots of positions, and have not been attached to them, and felt they could give them up at any time. If you could reach that state, that's also very advanced. My view is that the best thing you can do is say, "Look, I can take care of my family, I have enough clothes for whatever I want, my food bills are okay, I don't have to do anything more to maintain myself. Let me now become a highly principled individual." Maybe I made some compromises to get here and I'll pay for them somewhere along the way, but it's the sense of getting a handle on your desires that's the best thing I think most of us can aspire to.

I've seen executives who've said, "I will not act in a certain way anymore; I don't need to get higher in the organization." They've reached a level where they feel comfortable; they don't need to be the chairman, they don't need to be the CEO. That is very mature. Those are the people who help society, who suddenly, say, "I don't need this;" therefore, they can be people of principle. I think the biggest step in business is the understanding that attachments are a potentially corrupting influence. That's a very hard thing to say because most of us believe that attachments are the measure of success, and that's really the understanding that we have to get across to business, which is not to ask them to give up these things, because that's impractical. Rather, to ask them to remember that if you have these, you are suspect. You have weaknesses. These are weaknesses, and they can be used against you subtly or overtly, and that's what you have to be careful about. That's my point of view. It would be nice for everybody to be unattached, but let's face it—that's not going to happen.

There was a movement in the 1970s—in fact, it's still around, and there's been a book written about it called Voluntary Simplicity. *The book was republished just a few years ago because there is still a large segment of the population that continues to reach a certain point and say, Well, this is it, I don't need this. I've done it. I really want to live in a rural area and give up three cars and live more simply, and this is what I'm going to do.*

I think simplicity is always a good idea. I would also like some of them to stay in the corporation, or wherever their business is, and say, "I have enough for my lifestyle. Now my goal is to increase the standards of this corporation, because now I am free of the desire to accumulate more." Instead of leaving and living the quiet life, I would prefer they stayed and raised the standard. I think that would be the harder thing, and probably the more productive thing for the business and society as a whole.

Or to take the corporation and the employees and relocate to a more rural area.

I do not think location is the issue. What I'm looking for is people in the middle and senior level who feel they've reached where they want to be, who are well established, who do good work, and now devote themselves, in addition to their work, to raising the standards of conduct in the corporation. Now they can do that because they've come to a point where they feel they've put a hold on their attachments. If they stay in the fray and do more of that, I think they could be very helpful to the rest of us.

I worked for a large corporation for a number of years, and one of the things that happened in that corporation, and I saw it in many other corporations, was that the people who were giving you a promotion, which involves your having to relocate, having to uproot your family, having to move to a strange area, having to do all these things—they did that, and they expect you to do that. It's like, to draw the line is to put a halt on your career, on your advancement. What about that? Does that still exist?

Now when you say to somebody that I'm not going to move, I can plateau my career here, you may be doing it for purely self-ish reasons—because you don't like the climate or the moving inconvenience. But if you are doing it for your spiritual and family life, then you are saying, I am now going to stress the growth of my spirit and my soul and not so much the growth of my corporate success. That's the trade-off people have to continually make. The question is, Is that important to an individual? The more individuals we have who are making the choice that the growth of their spirit is just as important as the growth of their economic well-being, the better it is going to be for business ethics. Until people make that choice, the whole question of business ethics becomes a matter of legal definition. It's when individuals make a choice that the growth of their spirit is just as important as the growth of their economic well-being that the ethics of any society, not only business, benefits.

I know your focus is business, but I just want to say that I think the same idea can be applied to the political arena as well. The soul is almost totally absent in the political spectrum.

Oh, absolutely. Actually, I'm more interested in this whole concept being put before educators and the people who educate as much as I am in business, because the idea is that violence to the spirit is as detrimental as violence to the body. As a matter of fact, you can make a case that it's violence to the spirit that starts before violence to the body occurs, and that's something we don't pay much attention to. The idea of people in politics looking at the growth of their spirit and the spirit of the people around them is far more important. The whole idea here is to grow the spirit of our people. When you even think back to Roosevelt: "We have nothing to fear but fear itself," that was a call to the spirit of the United States. When Churchill said in WWII, "I have nothing to offer, but blood, sweat, and tears," again that was a call to the spirit of the people—not to their monetary well-being. It takes a certain kind of person to call somebody to their spirit, because first of all you have to be able to call to your own spirit before you can call to somebody else's. That's the dilemma we face.

With recent presidents, I would say John Kennedy had more of that sense of calling to the spirit than any recent president I can remember.

Kennedy and Reagan had the rhetorical skill to do it, but not at the level of Roosevelt because he had the more complete package. The ability to call to the goodness in human beings is an essential component of great leadership. To call to the spirit of a person. To do that, you have to work on your own spirit. And that's the thing that our political leaders miss—they are not working on their own spirit.

When you look at the educational structure that most of them come out of, it's one that leans heavily to the linear and the rational and not much to the philosophical or spiritual. It's mostly oriented to professions, careers, and career-building. I'm sure in your training as an engineer you didn't take many philosophy courses.

That's a very good point. In engineering there are problems, and usually there is a single solution to a problem, and you get brought up in that discipline. Dealing with problems that have clear solutions is the way most of us are taught. Spiritual knowledge, unless you are in a religious order, is essentially a self-motivated, self-study effort.

We also carry over this idea that we can completely solve problems in the social arena. Most of our social problems are beyond solution. All we can hope for is to improve their condition and point them in the right direction and be humble in our ideas for their solution.

I'd like to ask you about secrecy in business. Again, one of the traits of business is to maintain business secrecy about how we do things and how we make a profit, how we manufacture something, and so on. In your book A Higher Standard of Leadership, *one of the commitments you dwelt on, inspired by Gandhi's life and work, was this area of being willing to stand up to scrutiny.*

There are two parts to the secrecy issue, I believe. One is combined with being truthful. Gandhi always said that if you are being truthful and nonviolent, you can't have secrets, because having secrets is sort of a violation of that idea. Now in business, there are legitimate secrecy issues when you are negotiating a merger—and legal issues. Let's eliminate that kind of thing. But leaders as a whole have to have their lives open, because openness promotes trust. You share things with people you trust. You hide things from people you don't trust. In a very elementary sense, if you hide things from the people you are supposed to lead, then you don't trust them, and then they don't trust you. It's a natural phenomenon to be open with people you lead.

There is another side of that which says that people who get information have a responsibility to truth, so they should not use that information in an untruthful or violent sense. The example I would give is, if I give you a lot of information about myself and then you selectively use pieces of it out of context to ridicule me or put me down, then you are violating a principle, and then I am going to be less open with you. We have a vicious cycle that goes on. The people who use the information are as guilty of promoting secrecy as the people who have the information.

If you talk to any business executive or politician, they'll say, "Well, if I tell them everything, they'll misuse it." With justification as we've seen on many television and radio programs and the newspapers, they will misuse it to the person's disadvantage. Now we have created a vicious cycle. It's a responsibility on the user's part and on the person who has the information. There is also a responsibility on those of us who listen. We also have to say, "Wait a minute, this is not the whole truth." We, too, have to exercise better judgment. A leader who wants to lead his people in a positive sense and create a group of people who are committed has to minimize secrecy, because secrecy creates distrust, and trust is the foundation of good leadership. Without trust, you don't have anything.

We all have responsibility for this problem of eliminating secrecy. It is no use just being an investigative reporter running around saying, "You shouldn't have any secrets." When you get the information, if you use it improperly, then you are encouraging secrecy. This is something that the profession of journalism and others have not recognized—that the way they use information encourages secrecy. I've been on the side where you give analytical information to an executive, and they use part of it to justify themselves—you give it to another side (for example, environmentalists), they use another part to justify themselves. It's the same set of information, but nobody will project all the information for the public. They'll use only the portion that justifies their idea, and that encourages secrecy. So we are all guilty in the circle. We all should take responsibility for the fact that we have encouraged secrecy.

The media essentially is oriented to sound bites, and so the average in-depth news report on the evening news on television is going to be 90 seconds in duration, not very in-depth. You can't do much in 90 seconds. So many of these issues are very complex—with multilayered, multileveled possibilities. They can't be addressed in the way the media for the mass public is operated.

There are two levels. One is that our issues are complex, and that certainly is something to think about, but then it's also how they treat individuals. When they treat individuals with these half-truths, then you're really in trouble, because then all individuals shy away from the media, and the result is secrecy, which breeds the investigative reporter who is trying to ferret out the so-called truth, which is a misnomer for what they try to do. But they ferret it out, and then again you get half a story. There is a cycle now that has developed where the truth is obscure.

There is also this idea that you get what you're looking for, so if you go into a story looking for a particular end point to the story and you have that in mind beforehand, then you are going to do everything to try to find that. That's what I think is the basic flaws of investigative reporting, since it is often predicated on the idea that something is very wrong here.

We don't want to find something that's good, because that wouldn't make a story. It's that old analogy of "blood leads." In the television profession, they say that if you can find a crime with blood, you don't have to do an in-depth analysis. There is somebody lying on the street bleeding.

We can almost call the '90s the "bleed decade"—particularly the way the mass media, the electronic media, has done with so much of the sensationalism.

Right. This encourages the secrecy mentality. It's kind of unfortunate, because the press thinks they are trying to create something open, but unfortunately they are creating more secrecy because more people are shying away. So you see, it's that cycle that has unfortunately developed. It's a question of being antagonistic, which we like—we like the competitive aspect of life, which can create an antagonistic attitude.

Prior to General Electric getting out of the weapons business, they owned National Broadcasting Company, NBC. So when they were in the midst of making nuclear weapons, I don't think you were going to find in-depth reports on nuclear weapons manufacturing in America on NBC.

GE still owns NBC. I think that the more interesting question is the one that happened on *Dateline*, when they blew up that truck. What was interesting was that nobody did an in-depth investigative report on television on how that whole thing happened. If it had been a politician who told such an untruth on television, they would have nailed him or her with a barrage of investigative reporting. It was handled internally.

It seems that there is an unwritten law of the media: You don't report on one another.

That is true. It would be unfair to single out the media. All the professions have the same code. The media and the profession of journalism, because of their First Amendment protection, have a special role and, therefore, a special responsibility.

Doesn't it come back to principles and morals and how you live your life? How can you separate how you live your life from how you operate your business? But yet, that's what we've done in large part.

In one of the first sections of my book is the idea of a single standard of conduct. Gandhi was emphatic in not compartmentalizing his life and conduct. But we have developed a scheme that says you treat your friends one way, and you work in business another way. And that creates a very slippery slope of expediency. So once you get on that slope, then you can compromise anything to get something done. We now have this principle of, let's just get it done. Nike even has a commercial, "Just do it." It's the principle, get it done, and then they don't care how it's done. And that's the dilemma of this double standard of conduct. For my friends, my family, I'm going to have one standard, and getting ahead in business requires a different standard. Once you get on that different standard, you are in trouble. Because then how far low will you go? And then, won't it influence your conduct at home? I mean, these are connected. You can't separate your spirit in two parts.

Right. That's really what we're talking about. The soul of business. The soul of how we function in business.

When people talk about the spirit and soul of business, we have to remember that the focus has to be the individual. It's the soul of individuals. The more individuals we have in a business who work there because their spirit is in the business and who are looking for growth in their spirit, the better the business will be. It's the spirit of the individuals that combine together to make an organization. Organizations don't have souls. Individuals have souls.

So this is where the synergy comes in. One plus one is three.

Right. If your spirits are together, one plus one is three. It's the Greeks at Thermopylae. It's the same idea that small groups of people can do great things because their spirits are together, their ideals are together, their hearts are together—not just because their minds are together. That's the key.

Do you want to give us a little story about why the Greeks at Thermopylae are important?

Because it's a small group of people who took on a large army in a particular situation, held them off, and saved their city, and it really shows that a small group of determined people willing to lay down their lives can overcome very great odds. There are countless examples of this, and you can see it in business. There is a company in Finland called Nokia that makes cellular phones. They are the number-two cellular phone maker in the world after Motorola. How did this outfit in Finland get to be this big?

Small companies with determination and spirit have successfully challenged large established companies. Who would have thought Honda could have challenged General Motors? Small resources with a great heart become large resources. So the concept of commitment and the concept of the spirit, having a challenge, the concepts of creativity and high energy that come from all that can overcome great odds. That's the lesson that goes throughout history—small groups of people bonded together in spirit overcoming great odds.

I think Finland is an interesting country to point to because it is a small population, yet their averages for everything compared to other countries are so much higher. I think part of it is the climate. People have to survive a very harsh winter there and have to deal with challenges other people do not have to deal with. Everybody pitches in together. There is a sense of community in Finland.

And that is one of the real dilemmas of large countries: how to create senses of community within large countries.

Don't you have to do it on a regional basis?

The old problem is if you do it regionally, you still need to maintain the unity of the nation. This is one of the dilemmas of the popular movement of diversity. You see, I come at it from a different angle. I always say the first thing you ought to worry about is unity—unity of the human spirit. Because if you stress diversity, then people think their spirits are different, which is incorrect. The spirit is the same. Diversity is on the surface.

If you identify with the oneness of spirit, then diversity is not a problem.

It almost becomes irrelevant in the discriminatory context. What is happening today is we are stressing diversity so much without emphasizing the foundation, which is that the spirit is unified underneath. It's become the popular thing to do—encourage and stress diversity. My thought is that we should encourage the unity of spirit first, and then diversity won't be a continuous issue because I will think of you as diverse, and enjoy the diversity. It won't be an issue to me because underneath I'll know we are the same.

Speaking again of that diversity and also the culture of region-alism having an identity in the smaller areas, there is so much hap-pening in our society, our culture, since areas and communities are being impacted by new buildings, new businesses coming in. A Wal-Mart coming into a community is not only the Wal-Mart com-ing in—it's bringing in a whole truckload of baggage with it, of other kinds of businesses, plus it's going to impact the community in ways that the community doesn't really see at the moment, but it's going to happen downstream where smaller businesses can't compete. It seems there is so much going on that challenges the sense of community.

There are a lot of factors working against the community. The only thing that seems to be working in its favor right now is some of this electronic communication—the Internet. This is still in the future.

I recently saw a poster that said, "A sense of community may be roadkill on the information highway."

Actually, I am somewhat optimistic. The "information high-way" can be used to create this bond to develop the community. With video, voice, and data in real time, we can do it—we can create emotional and spiritual bonds. The question is, Will we? A sense of community requires people to connect in their spirit. There is a theory now that says that since you and I share infor-mation, we have a sense of community. It has to be much more than that. The only way you develop a sense of community is to share emotion and spirit. The "information highway" can be used to develop this sense of community. Will it be used? It is proba-bly too early to tell. It does have the potential. A family has a sense of community—not because it shares information—it has a sense of community because of the spiritual, emotional bond between them.

It's true. I have the experience, probably a fortunate and an unusual experience, of being on a network that is based on a spiritual tradition, so the people on it that are communicating on the network are all people who have had this experience, so the level of communication is very high, and it's also got a spiritual base. The spiritual base, of course, has to happen first before the other can happen.

The higher the level of spiritual attachment, the higher the quality of information transfer. It is important to recognize that a lot of what they talk about in business these days, like empowerment and teams, will only work in the long run if people have common objectives, common spiritual and emotional needs. Otherwise, it's just a question of getting together with one group for one week and then leaving them and going to another group for another week. That doesn't create any emotional bonding.

One of the things that's happening in organizations today that people are not talking about is that we are asking our workers to be more flexible, more educated, and more adaptable to change. Everybody is talking about wonderful opportunities from change and flexibility. Everybody is telling us to get rid of bureaucracy. But bureaucracy has some wonderful attributes to it. One of them is stability. Bureaucracy brings stability to people's lives. People know what they are getting; the future is predictable. They can bring up their children in a systematic manner. If you want to think of the old TV ideal of Ward Cleaver in *Leave It to Beaver.* Ward Cleaver needed a stable environment. If he was in for a lot of change, it would have been much harder to bring up his family.

Bureaucracy has many problems; it stifles people, and so on. This flexible organization that we are talking about with lots of change and new careers and that sort of stuff has its own problems. And it's creating a lot of hardship on employees and their families and in their abilities to nurture and bring up children, because there is no stability to their careers now. This is something people are not talking about. They are talking about the opportunity part. But they are not talking about the aspect of instability in people's lives and families, and their ability to create a stable social structure. It is not going to go away—it's going to stay because that's the reality. Just like bureaucracy came and it had its own problems. The flexible, adaptive organization has its own issues. We should discuss both sides and try to alleviate the negative impacts.

But what are the ethics of a business that's making huge profits, and yet they're still downsizing?

I think the statistics say that 50 percent of the businesses that downsize do not increase their profits. Most of it makes little sense. What businesses have to do is to organize themselves to do the business that is required. Downsizing by itself doesn't do anything. You have to figure out what you want to do and then get the right number of people to do it. Now sometimes it's true that there are some organizations that have more people than needed because the system allowed it to grow that way. What are the ethics of laying people off? I categorize this under a general class of problems where you have two principles that you like, which are in conflict. I think we talked about this earlier. This is the fundamental challenge of leadership. It's what I call duality. There is a whole set of dualities.

I borrowed this idea from Alan Watts. Dualities are things that you cannot separate like both ends of a pole. For example, a leader has to be *above* the people he leads, and he has to be *of* the people that he leads. This is a kind of duality. Above them *and* of them. It is the word *and* that captures the duality. Think of a general in the army. For example, General Schwarzkopf in the Gulf War. On the one hand, he wants to be one of the soldiers, but he can't take the same risk as the soldiers. He is not in the battlefield; he is at the command post in the bunker. So what does Schwarzkopf do? He's a wise individual. He recognizes that he cannot go out on the battlefield because that is a level of risk his country does not want him to take. As a matter of fact, his soldiers don't want him killed because he's their leader. So he wears battle fatigues, eats in the mess hall, he tries to be as much a part of them as he can without being allowed to share their risk. He acknowledges that the ordinary soldier under his command is making the greater sacrifice. This is an example of a leader who understands this particular duality and is effective in dealing with it.

If you're the CEO, you have a corner office, you have a limo, you have various perks, and the hierarchy puts you above others. Now to lead properly, you also have to be of them. So you are in a constant dilemma. Because if you are too much of them, then you lose your authority. If you are too much above them, then people think you are up there and don't care about them. This tension exists whether you are president of the U.S. or whether you are a corporate executive. It is only when you have a truly integral life, like Gandhi, that you don't have this tension.

Do you see business as being a place where it can be the catalytic agent for real transformation of the social arena?

I guess I would have to say only partially. I think in the long run that businesses have a central purpose of survival as an organization. If you have a central purpose of surviving as an organization, I don't think the organization can bear the primary responsibility for uplifting society. I believe individuals in business, as citizens, bear the responsibility, and they can guide their organizations to participate.

EPILOGUE

Again we are reminded of the importance of service as a means of tapping into the soul of work. Using Gandhi as a model, Keshavan Nair explores the process of making decisions, setting goals, and implementing actions guided by the spirit of service and commitment to values that is essential. He tells us that it is possible to apply spiritual principles in the workplace and to thrive. Drawing on the actual experience of Gandhi, Nair challenges each of us to step beyond our cultural conditioning and learn new ways to hold and use power, while at the same time seeking a universal work ethic.

✦ CHAPTER SEVEN ✦

Business and the Future Society

Willis Harman and Michael Toms

PROLOGUE

*T*he world as we have known it is transforming before our eyes.
The old rules don't apply any longer, as we watch institutional structures dissolve and reform themselves in search of a new
worldview. There is a major transition unfolding, and although it
may appear chaotic at times, a certain order emerges.

Willis Harman (1917–1997) was one of those people whose
life traversed this extraordinary shift, and who has continually
been a pioneer in helping us to better understand the changing
worldview. Willis was president of the Institute of Noetic Sciences
in Sausalito, California, up until 1996. For 16 years, Dr. Harman
was a senior social scientist at SRI International (formerly known
as Stanford Research Institute) in Menlo Park, California. He was
a founding member of the World Business Academy and emeritus
professor of engineering economic systems at Stanford University.

For the decade of 1980 to 1990, he was a member of the Board of Regents of the University of California. His books include Creative Work, *co-authored with John Horman;* Global Mind Change; *and he was the co-author of* Changing Images of Man *and* Higher Creativity.

MICHAEL TOMS: *Willis, at the root of this change is consciousness. In what ways do you see human consciousness and our perceptions changing?*

WILLIS HARMAN: Two things are happening, I think. With regard to consciousness, more and more individuals are perceiving in a different way. Also, consciousness as a topic, consciousness as something that we now recognize, was inadvertently left out of Western science. We are gaining new knowledge about consciousness as it relates to Western science.

What kind of new knowledge are we gaining?

The Institute of Noetic Sciences and various other organizations have been working for a good many years on topics relating to the relationship of the mind to healing, for example, and creativity and intuition and creative altruism, and so on. But what has been happening in more recent years is that we're becoming aware that we need to know more about this. We not only need to be more conscious, but we need to know more about consciousness in the scientific worldview. It becomes apparent that somehow this got left out, and that we have put together a worldview in which consciousness was omitted for perfectly good reasons several centuries ago. We've tried to live by this worldview as though it represented reality, and it's increasingly clear that it doesn't do a very good job at that.

In the book called Leadership and the New Science, *Margaret Wheatley took many of the emerging ideas and insights coming from quantum physics and applied them to the organizational world. Again, it's the old science versus the new science and how the rules change dramatically.*

There are interesting parallels. The old science versus the in-between science in the sense that quantum physics, for example, makes it rather clear that you can't leave out of the picture the consciousness of whoever is observing whatever it is you are studying. At the same time, that's not going all the way to really revising science in such a way that it includes consciousness as a causal factor in the overall picture. Each of us in our own individual lives operates as though what goes on in our minds could change things. In science, we pretend that that's not a factor. The net result is that we have a science that is extremely good at prediction and control, generating technologies. But it's not very good when you try to extend that picture to where it says anything about human beings and their relationship to the whole thing.

In the paradigm of science and human consciousness, somehow human consciousness dropped away so somehow we don't see it. Is this something that goes back to the time of the 17th century, when science split from the church?

Yes, I think very much so. Remember, there wasn't any such thing as a scientist at that time. The word hadn't even been coined. That small group that was trying to explore this new way of looking into reality observed that the church was a powerful institution, and the scientific community was a small group without any power. And you certainly didn't want to ask for trouble. So it was perfectly reasonable that you should say, Look, we're going to study the things that are physically measurable, and we'll leave the mind and the soul and the spirit to the church. And that's fine for

a long, long time, but then eventually, science gets a lot of persua-
sive power in this society, and we are encouraged to believe that
the scientific worldview is the way things really are, and then
there's this discrepancy, because in our own lives we don't feel
that that's the way things are. And then it turns out that consciousness as a causal factor is, in a way, the very central issue in
whether the science that we have is going to be adequate for our
needs in the future.

*We hear a lot about the Big Bang, and, again, related to
consciousness, what preceded the Big Bang? Did consciousness precede the material of the Big Bang? And again, it points
out the question: Did material exist preconsciousness or post-
consciousness? It's a paradox.*

This may be treading on ground that's going to bring up a lot
of feelings. But as long as you advance in this way, let's continue.
If consciousness is a causal factor and it needs to be in the picture
all the way along, then you are not in a position of saying that consciousness evolved and eventually it became what it is with human
beings, after the cranium and the neural networks had developed
to a certain point. So there is one kind of picture of reality—that
consciousness evolved over billions of years and eventually
becomes what it is now.

Now there is an alternative picture that's been around much
longer and has a great deal to support it, also, and that is that evolution took place, but consciousness was not only there all along;
consciousness is in some sense even primary. There is nothing
incompatible between that and the scientific explorations that we
have. But there's something psychologically very disturbing about
the fact that this is a major change in the way we look at the kind
of scientific knowledge we have. I think we are at a point in history where much of the culture is shifting over to a view of putting
consciousness and spirit in a much more central place, but we still

have the official view taught in all of our schools that it's at the end of the evolutionary path rather than at the beginning.

How would we equate that pre-existing consciousness with the concept of God?

I think God is the word that has been used to point in that general direction, but it's been used for a lot of other purposes, too— one of the most important of which is a dimension of people's individual experience. It's a word where people put meaning into it out of their own experience and their own concepts, but it certainly isn't just this. I think you can make a connection between the word *God* and the idea that the Universe started—not with the Big Bang, but with a great thought.

I want to shift into one of the places where the shift is happening in a large way. That is in the world of the corporate sector. If we look around us, we see these giant corporate mergers happening, as in early 1996 with Turner and Disney and Time Warner coming together. We have these globe-girdling corporate behemoths that seem to be beyond the government structures, and they are affecting our lives in major ways. What about that? What is your view?

It may seem as though you suddenly switched subjects, but I don't think that's so. I think there is a very intimate connection between the changing worldview and the challenge that's being faced by the corporate world, or the challenge that it will increasingly face. We have large corporations, as you say, girdling the globe—and with tremendous power—and that power is not under any control. It's kind of a wild power. It responds to various financial signals, but it's not responsible to the people in the sense that a democratic government is responsible to the people. Yet in some ways it represents more power.

At the same time that all of that's happening, you have the

actions of corporations clearly not always in the public good—corporations moving out of communities and essentially destroying them. Having downsizing and layoffs and masses of people in trouble, environmental results from their actions. Now one temptation is to blame the people in business for their values, and that doesn't really make much sense, because if any of us were elevated to those positions, we would behave in the same way because we are part of a system, and it's the system values and the system logic that are being responded to. I think we are at a point where the legitimacy of that tremendous amount of power represented by the world capitalistic structure is being challenged just as surely, although not as strongly yet, as the power of world communism was challenged prior to 1991. When world communism disappeared within a week, we were surprised, but if we had been carefully watching the signs, the legitimacy challenge, we might not have been. And similarly here.

When I talk to business groups, I have on occasion asked them, if world capitalism, this network of tremendous corporations and financial structures—if the legitimacy of that were being challenged similar to the way world communism was challenged in the early '80s in the Soviet Union, very, very quietly, would you be looking at the right signals to notice? Would you even see that? I want to emphasize that this is not an anti-business sentiment. I'm a founding member of the World Business Academy. We are trying to create dialogues around these important topics. Part of what has happened is businesses started with charters that essentially said that the businesses were to operate in the public good, and they had a charter that gave them certain privileges because they were operating in the public good. You'll find that as the idea of the responsibility of the business to the stockholders primarily has gotten stronger and stronger, the concept of corporations acting primarily in the public good went by the wayside. That is part of the challenge. Part of the challenge has to do with environmental sustainability. Part of it has to do with systemic injustices in the sense of power versus lack of power in the world. You hear this particularly from the Third World countries. We're at a time that the worldview is shifting—modern society is shifting in important ways—and because businesses and corporations are so much at the heart of that, they are of necessity at the heart of this transformation.

Speaking of the changes, one of the things that occurred, not to many people's notice, was that countries got off the gold and silver standard in their money, and so now money is based on the strength of how strong the country is, not so much how much gold they have in Fort Knox. What about that as a shift?

I think it's an interesting example of how important things can happen without our noticing. In the early 1970s, all the major currencies in the world shifted from a gold and silver base over to what they call "fiat" currency—that is, currency that is based on faith. At the same time, the amount of money in the world began to expand tremendously and rapidly. It turns out that when you borrow from a bank on a line of credit, you are creating money. The bank, for a certain amount of solid assets, can loan much more money than that, because not everybody is going to make their claims at the same time. So you have a tremendous amount of money sloshing around the world, and very little of it anymore has to do with goods and services. If you go back 30 or 40 years ago, the world economy consisted of a lot of separate economies with some links, and was primarily an economy of goods and services. The economy today (of the international money flows) is primarily an economy of speculation with less than 5 percent of it having anything to do with goods and services. I think it's anybody's guess where this is all going. Many writers and analysts have been raising the question recently: What happens to all this? Where is it headed? And what does it do to people, as well as what does it do to the natural environment?

What is your view of the Federal Reserve? The Federal Reserve is made up of bankers and businessmen. It is not a government agency. It operates separately from the government, and the members are not subject to election. They seem to operate in some separate domain. How do you view it?

I think that's true. They are not a government agency. They are not totally private, either. They have some responsibilities. They have the authority to create money. Rather than look at a particular institution like that, you can't really answer the question: Is a corporation good or bad, or is the Federal Reserve bank good or bad? It all depends on what values are operative. And behind all of this, most of the traditional values have kind of lost their power because they were based on a picture of reality, a religious worldview, that was the source of their ultimate authority, in a way. Now as science appeared to weaken our religious concepts, it also weakened the values that were based in those. Whereas those played an important role in making capitalism really work well for a while, as those values weakened, and the economic values, financial values, material values began to get stronger by comparison, the same institutions work less well, and the legitimacy is more in question. All of these things connect together in a way that I know is kind of befuddling to people when they try to think of them all at once, but you can't separate the changing values from the institutional crisis from what happens in science.

You've been involved in the World Business Academy now since it started in 1987. What progress have you seen?

Some of the questions that were very difficult to raise five or ten years ago are much easier to raise nowadays. One example is, there have been several conferences of people in business recently around the issue of spirit in the workplace, spirit in business. These are not places where people go together just to kind of feel good and talk about the spiritual aspects of their lives. They are really asking why we can not have a spiritually enriching environment, a spiritually enriching institution in which to carry out a very important part of our lives—which is our professional work.

If you pursue this question, you get to the same place that you'll get to if you pursue any other important social question. There are characteristics of the whole system now that are causing institutional breakdown anyplace you turn. None of our institutions are working well now. When you try to get underneath that, you find that those institutions rest upon a collective belief system into which you and I and everybody else is buying in. It's only as we begin to question that belief system that we'll begin to bring about this overall system change. The more understanding you have of that, the more clear it becomes what any individual can do or what can be done by any small organization or group of people.

That may explain why we have a Gallup Poll that says that 80 percent of Americans are dissatisfied with their work.

I think that's a big factor.

That's a pretty major statistic. That dissatisfaction is perhaps the beginning of the questioning.

I think it is. I think we don't always identify the right target for the questioning. The first temptation is to find the scapegoat somewhere, to blame the executives that are high in the business system, or some people in government, or somewhere outside of ourselves. Eventually we have to come back to saying, really, the source of all of this is in this collective belief system that we've been buying into, and we simply have to replace it with a different one. I think that's what is going on.

Speaking of collective belief systems, there is a belief that 5 percent unemployment is acceptable, which means several millions of people out of work is acceptable. This, of course, is based on the old model, right? Why can't we have more jobs? Certainly there is a lot of work to be done. Why can't we create more jobs? For instance, there's a lot of work to be done cleaning up the toxic waste dumps, but the work doesn't happen.

There is no end to the work that can be done for the common good. It doesn't all easily fit into forms that can make a profit in the profit-making part of the economy, and that has become dominant. We are working against ourselves in a peculiar way. We believe in labor productivity and substituting machines for human labor and getting more and more done with fewer and fewer person-hours. Also, we believe in unending economic growth. So the economy has to grow at a certain rate. We've now gotten to the point where almost the only way we can conceive of someone relating to this society is to have a job in it or be married to somebody who has a job or be studying to get a job. As long as we are in that bind, we're saying we've got to have more and more growth, because we've got to have more and more jobs, but at the same time all of that growth is creating increasing environmental sustainability problems. It can't go on growing forever. We really are at a point where literally we don't know what to do, because what we try to accomplish in one direction undercuts what we are trying to accomplish in another direction. It's not as simple as just environment versus jobs, but that points to a very real dilemma.

I'm sure you will remember back in the '60s in California and elsewhere in the United States, there was a great deal of discussion about how much leisure time we were going to have in the future. This was used to sell second homes and retirement possibilities. And yet we come down the pike 25 to 30 years later, and we see that not only is there no leisure time, people are working longer hours at fewer jobs.

That is one of the ways in which the institutions are breaking down. I don't think we should look upon this as a time in which we wring our hands and speak words of despair to each other. It's sort of like adolescence. I remember my adolescence as a fairly painful time. But if I look at it as going from childhood to maturity—or maybe not maturity—at least adulthood, I view it very differently. I think that's the period that we are in now. What we've been calling the modern world, in some very fundamental ways, will not work in the long term. It will not work in terms of environmental sustainability; it won't work in terms of the separation of the rich/poor, both within countries and between north and south or developed and developing countries. It will not work in terms of its marginalization, pushing off to the edges so many people and cultures. It doesn't work because it doesn't have a worldview that fits with our total experience. And so we are moving toward a society that is more satisfactory in all these dimensions, but because it's like adolescence, it's a painful time.

Is all this growth good? It strikes me that some of the emphasis on growing seems to create a lot of the problems that we wind up having downstream. The environment is one example, jobs another. Growth, more growth. We've got to keep the gross national product happening. We've got to keep that percentage moving up. We've got to keep the Dow moving, et cetera. Can you address that question: Is growth good?

There was a time when we would not raise the question whether growth in the human population of the earth was good or not because it wasn't necessary to raise it. Now we kind of agree that it's got to level off someplace. I think you can say much the same thing about the growth in the amount of economic activity. What's the purpose of economic product? Fundamentally, the purpose has to be to add richness to the human life. And yet when we look at the economy today, the purpose of more economic product is politically to make sure that we don't have rising unemployment, and financially it's to add to the riches of many people who already have a fair amount. It's being questioned in a way that 30 years ago you'd never have heard economic growth questions.

Of course, if you go back farther, it wasn't even defined, and it wasn't an issue. It's a fairly recent idea that the individual corporation has to grow to an unlimited extent and that the economy has to grow to an unlimited extent, and yet clearly, this can't happen. Just mathematically, exponential functions can't grow forever. They do level off. They either level off or they crash. So you have to get behind that and say, Where did we get this idea that all of this growth is important? Why can you not have a healthy economy where the amount of economic product remains more or less the same? It relates very much to this basic set of beliefs. It's included within those beliefs that productivity is unqualifiedly good, technological advance is good, economic growth is good, competition is good, that having more and more of this society run by economic logic and by economic values and having the economy be more and more the paramount institution in this society— that all of that is the direction of what we've been calling progress.

What's being called into question is all of that together—not just one factor of it. And the reason it's being called into question is because if you look carefully, that set of assumptions is not compatible with the kinds of social goals that we all pretty much agree we want. We want a certain kind of a society for our grandchildren to live in. We want the environment preserved enough. We want them to have enough resources so that they are not wanting, so that they have the same kinds of chances that we had. Those two sets of things are not compatible, it turns out. It's not an obvious conclusion. But that's one way of illustrating the predicament that we are in. But you can't just look at that, because you also have to look at what you started with when we began to converse, this changing worldview. We're saying there was an ecological, spiritual, soft-value, feminist kind of dimension that had been left out of modern society, and we need to reclaim that. And as we reclaim that, we reassess all these other assumptions.

I can understand how people get confused when they try to think about this all at once. But at the same time, we know that organic systems do go through major changes, and when they do, there is a kind of chaos and reformation. Sort of like the chaos that exists between the phase of the caterpillar and the butterfly. It may seem uncomfortable to be conscious of being in that chaos period, but that's probably the best way to look at where we are.

The caterpillar actually liquefies to become the butterfly, so we may be in the liquefying state. That's a difficult one, sometimes, to bear.

At the same time, in the caterpillar there are certain cells that the biologist calls "imaginal cells," and those cells seem to know how to multiply and form a little piece of the adult insect. They seem to know how to do that. It's built in there somewhere—not necessarily in the genes, but somehow in the whole organism. So these "imaginal cells" then create little pieces of the adult insect, which then come together and become the whole.

Now I think you can see something like that happening in our society already. New Dimensions Radio, the Institute of Noetic Sciences, alternative economies, alternative communities, eco-feminist movements, and so on—all of those are illustrations of little groups of people getting together to try to create a piece of the new society that we sense is coming.

Are you hopeful about the future society?

I don't see any reason not to be. The earth has made it this far. Evolution has made it this far. We can't really be in much trouble, can we?

But one of the worldviews that operates quite consistently in these times is the support of cynicism and pessimism. Somehow if you are thinking hopefully or optimistically, there is something wrong with that thinking because it doesn't account for what's really happening.

Let's make a distinction. There's a foolish kind of optimism. If you look out there and say, Well, everything's going fine—it isn't. Of course it isn't. But if you mean by optimism, the sense that just as we as individuals somehow know how to start from a single fertilized cell and become a Michael Toms or a Willis Harman, this human society knows how to become a really human society—that's in our collective mind somehow. We sense it. We know the right values. It's just that we don't seem to know how to get there. Optimism is the sense of a deep trust that together we do know where we're going, even though we don't know exactly how to write books about it and put on newscasts about it. That deep trust is the healthiest attitude you can have toward life. But it's not a foolish optimism. It doesn't say that we may not have to go through some trying times to get where we are headed.

In your book An Incomplete Guide to the Future—*a wonderful book, which was one of the books that really grabbed me when I first saw it in the late '70s—I was really struck by the title, and there was a sense that you couldn't possibly write a complete guide to the future, anyway. Just that sense of birthing. In your own personal life, how do you deal with your own human consciousness and your own spiritual path? Do you have a spiritual path? Do you have a spiritual practice?*

I've certainly had a spiritual practice. I find that now my work is my practice because I'm spending all my time doing both what enriches me, what informs me, and what is totally delightful.

So you see your work as your practice.

Yes. I think maybe one could almost generalize from that. Because we start off without much help toward finding our essence, our true spiritual nature, we've created a bunch of institutions that pretty much get in the way of that. So because of that, a lot of people these days in their early adult life or mid-adult life feel this urge to discover themselves in a way and discover the dimensions that have somehow been suppressed—discover the resources that we can tap into if we simply open ourselves up. Discover that having total trust is not a foolish attitude, but one that's very well based. So that personal spiritual path, spiritual practice, whatever, at this point in history—that becomes an important aspect of one's life. But then you get to a point where you say, Well, I'm not totally spiritually evolved, but it feels as though I came here to do something. I'd better get with what I came to do. And that turns out to be mainly saying yes to your own intuitive sense of what it is. So you get led to the work that is the center of your life.

I can't answer the question of why work is the center of our lives, but it does seem to be the nature of human beings. There is a profound sense in which we have a deep sense of purpose, we have a sense of some work to do, and that's why we're here. Now it doesn't have to be something that makes headlines. It may be, for example, simply creating a home, a family environment within which wonderful things can happen. Whatever that work is, as you find it, and you put more and more of yourself into it, I find that there is no separation between that and spiritual practice.

I do believe that. How old are you, Willis?

I'm in my 78th year.

It's amazing how you are really out there with your energy and doing what you love to do. It's great.

I'll have to confess, I didn't really get clear what life was about until I was past 60, and I didn't really get clear what I was about until past 70. I'm a slow learner, granted. But I do think that we underestimate the richness of later life, and we do it collectively. We almost encourage the idea that you should retire from creative work and go sit on a bench in St. Petersburg or something. Quite the contrary. When you retire from the economy is when your real work should begin.

It seems as if your work is feeding you and encouraging you and empowering you to go forward. It's a good connection to make. It speaks to one of the changing paradigms of our society. I was reading an article the other day about how the baby boomers aren't going to allow themselves to be called "seniors." Again, this is an indication of a shifting worldview. How do we relate to what's happening?

I think we have had this very bad idea that your work is a job in the mainstream economy, and that's a big part of what we're getting over. Partly, because people are being forced to recognize that not everybody is going to have a job in the mainstream economy because the economy can't grow that fast. So, we're being forced to discover something that would be good to discover even if we weren't being forced to. There is a profound difference between your life work and your job. If in the latter part of your life they become one and the same thing, you are one of the very fortunate ones. But it doesn't really matter much. The work is what's important. And it's of central importance. It's not just a job to get income so you can go in and divert yourself with some sort of pleasures and numb yourself to what's really going on.

If you were to make a projection and have updates in your Incomplete Guide to the Future, *how do you see the future unfold-*

ing over the next few years, getting to the next millennium? What do you think some of the important things are that we might be wanting to look at?

I had occasion to go back and look at that book, which was written over 20 years ago, and there's very little in there that I would feel I had to change. It points in the direction that we've been talking about. It points in the direction of a changing picture of the nature of reality—more emphasis on the spiritual dimension. It points to raising the question about what the economy is really for, and is the economy really what society is about, or is the economy a tool that society should be using wisely in order to promote the common good?

I think the general conclusion I would draw from this is that because I was by no means the only one who was raising those questions at the time, and even 25 or 30 years back, there were some. I think what it points to is that at some level of ourselves, we really do know where we're going, and we really do know what we have to do to get there. As we can listen to that, we can maybe in little ways help others to see where we have to go. That's different from generating the collective will to go through that change. That's more where we are now.

It's apparent to literally tens of millions of people, fairly clearly now, the kinds of things in society that have to change, fundamental things, and the kind of society that we have to create together. It's more or less clear how we would have to work together to do that. What we have not gotten to yet is the sense of collective will to do that, and also getting over the fear when things change at that fundamental level, but nevertheless, as the trust deepens, the fear weakens. So we need collective will, and we need a deep trust. Then we've got it made.

I want to go back before your book, Incomplete Guide to the Future, *and refer to* Changing Images of Man, *which was the report that came out of SRI, and then later became a book. And that report strikes me as very visionary as far as what was going to happen. Can you explain how it was so visionary?*

Winston Franklin was at the Kettering Foundation at the time, and he came to us and asked us if we would work on this topic, and we had, as he well knew, some inclinations along those lines. So we put together this book of how the image of humans in the universe was going through some profound changes. There were already signs of that. And it also spelled out some of the implications of that. Now, interestingly enough, James Redfield came by to do a New Dimensions program and stopped by our office, and one of the questions that came up was: How did you come to write *The Celestine Prophecy?* And he said, Well, you know I ran across a report from SRI called "Changing Images of Man," and that got me thinking. So these things come together in very interesting ways.

That's a great story. I was just visualizing in my mind the changing images of man and the nine steps. I'm sure they are all there.

They're not spelled out as neatly as he did. It didn't have the readability, we'll have to admit that.

What about the activities of the World Business Academy? What has been accomplished? What are the future hopes there?

The World Business Academy and the Institute of Noetic Sciences and various other people and organizations are collaborating presently on a project that I think is one of the most exciting things I've ever been involved with. It's hard to conceive. What we are attempting to do is take all this wisdom that is distributed around in various individuals who have been looking at these things for quite a while and try to create a scenario which, in a certain sense, would be like an "existence theorem" in mathematics. That is, it would show that from where we are now, with all of its problems, to a desirable society, not just for a few people, but for everybody on the planet, that there is at least one pathway by which you could get from here to there. But in order to create that scenario, you have to imagine various kinds of legislation, changing incentive systems like tax laws, various kinds of new communities springing up, new energy sources, and so on. If we build all of those into one scenario, then, essentially, what that does is erase the despair; it gives us reason to think there is at least one and probably many ways to get there from here. And also any small group of people who are working on something can see how that fits into the whole. It's really part of a much vaster pattern. So that's one of the activities of the World Business Academy.

The other things that we do there are mainly trying to create—in one way or another—dialogue about these very important issues and about the central role of business in all of this. Because since business has become the dominant institution on the planet, it now has a responsibility that was never associated with business in the past. You know, you could say four or five decades ago, the business of business is business. And it seemed reasonable to people. It no longer seems reasonable at all. The business of business has to be the future of the planet, because it's such a dominant force in creating that future.

How is the academy going about that?

We have international meetings, we have local meetings, we have publications. You know, the same sorts of things every organization does to create the necessary dialogue.

It seems to me that one of the aspects of the future is more collaboration.

Absolutely. Once we have recognized that we really are inter-dependent, it only makes sense to work together. It does not make sense to try to beat out the other guy, because there is not such a thing, really, in this ultimate calculus of I win/you lose. I can only win when we all win.

So the changing paradigm may be from "I compete" to "I cooperate."

Yes, or I compete within a cooperative framework. Like sports. You compete in sports, but you are first agreed upon a framework within which you carry out that competition. Competition has its good aspects, but only (certainly only at the global level) if it's within a collaborative framework of how are we going to build together a global society that is going to surmount the kinds of problems that we have and that's really going to be worthy of us.

EPILOGUE

The late Willis Harman was a visionary whose life path always seemed to place him on the edge of the new—what was coming. In this dialogue, which occurred one year before his death, he raises questions that need to be asked, and points out that a new model of business is emerging. It will take time and the commitment of each one of us, but the old model is in its death throes. He also reminds us once again that work and spiritual practice go hand in hand. Whatever the work may be for you, as you discover it and put more of yourself into it, it will lead you to where you need to go.

CHAPTER EIGHT

Bringing Spirit to Work

Barry Schieber and Michael Toms

PROLOGUE

We enjoy more material prosperity than any society in the history of humanity, and yet so many people find work unsatisfying and stressful. Still, we spend one-third or more of our days working, and the quality of our experience there affects the rest of our time. Usually we assume that the perspectives of business or work and those of the spiritual path are incompatible, yet each may be able to contribute something valuable that is usually missing in the other. How can we blend the pragmatic aspects of work with the inner depths of the spiritual path? How can we learn to enjoy work and feel like we are making a contribution? How can we make work more meaningful and effective?

Barry Schieber is the former dean of the Nyingma Institute in Berkeley, California. He has an MBA from UC Berkeley and enjoyed a highly successful career as an investment advisor for some 20 years. While still acting in the business world, he trained with Tarthang Tulku Rinpoche, a Tibetan lama, for over 20 years. After leaving business, he spent five years in solitary retreat. He leads seminars and workshops and gives talks on mastering successful work.

MICHAEL TOMS: *Barry, perhaps it would be good to start out by just talking a little bit about the Nyingma Institute, because I am sure many of our readers are not familiar with it. What is it, and what does it do?*

BARRY SCHIEBER: Nyingma Institute was founded in 1973 by Tarthang Tulku, an accomplished Tibetan lama, with the purpose of spreading the compassion and wisdom of his tradition here in the West. We give evening courses and retreats throughout the year. We also do retreats in Europe and Brazil. We have quite a few people interested in coming from long distances to understand what we are teaching.

One of the things you teach is continuing legal education courses. Can you describe those?

We began that three years ago right after I came off my retreat. A member of our staff found out that in California, the legal profession needed to have continuing legal education units and asked if we should do something. So I said, Sure, let's go ahead and do something. Primarily we have a relaxation program called Kum Nye, which we have found to be very effective. Also, it is something I did daily for five years on my retreat, so I knew the benefits of it. We applied to the state bar to have the program accredited. Two weeks later they came back and said, Sure, go ahead. Then we were faced with this prospect of attracting attorneys in the San

Francisco Bay Area from a small meditation retreat center that used to be a fraternity house right next to the University of California, Berkeley. So we were very creative. We got the county law book that had everyone's picture in it, and we went through the book and said, Okay, who would be interested in this? We did it intuitively, and sure enough, 12 people came to this workshop.

Interestingly, the largest legal newspaper in the Bay Area came to give us a review. As you can well imagine, the review was going to be tilted toward, how could a small meditation center, of all places in Berkeley, give a course to relax lawyers? As it turned out, the reviewer loved our course and gave us an *A* rating. That began a program that has continued throughout the state of California, even into Texas and Colorado. Now we've even had corporations and state agencies that have heard about it and say, Could you come and give a stress-reduction course to us; we've heard good things about you. So I think it is one of the ways that Nyingma Institute has really expanded. It's been helpful for many people. The response has been quite favorable.

How did you yourself personally connect with this tradition and with Tarthang Tulku?

I think the easiest way to say it is that I heard about it; I was interested in meditation. I heard about Tarthang Tulku. At that time, he had just purchased the fraternity house that was being transformed into a meditation center. I went to take a class with him and sat in the back row, fell asleep quite often, and then slowly as I was very interested in what the teachings were, sort of woke up a little bit. I was asked to help, and before I knew it I was helping quite a bit. Then I had the opportunity to take a long retreat, which was the most beneficial thing I have ever done. Then I began to say this was something very worthwhile, and I'd like to continue doing it. It wasn't in my original career plan, I can tell you that.

How does one decide to do a five-year retreat?

It's very awesome. It was only three years. But I think it was because of lack of spiritual progress that I was there five years. The first person that took his retreat was told it would be only a few months, and it was only after six months that he realized that this was a three-year retreat. So it's very gradually step by step, until you get acclimated to the water.

I don't think many of our readers have had anything close to such an experience. What was it like for you?

It was initially quite a different experience because I have always been more outgoing and social. For the most part, I spent most of my time alone. It was difficult for quite a while. I couldn't say that any day went by that I said, Oh boy, this is really a breeze or that I learned to levitate. Basically it was very challenging. Then I had the good fortune of tending some roses. I really think the gardening aspect of it opened my perspective completely. I became an avid rose gardener and designed some gardens. So the meditation and the roses and a beautiful setting all were very beneficial. It was just a wonderful experience, though it was difficult for quite a while.

So let's talk a little bit about this book Mastering Successful Work.

The first sentence tells you quite a bit. "Since I came to this country 25 years ago, work has been perhaps my greatest teacher." I think this is quite a statement.

Does this come from Tarthang Tulku's experience?

Exactly. Here was a very well-trained, highly accomplished Tibetan lama who came to the United States, became a US citizen, worked with us for 25 years, nonstop—long, long hours. He said that this has been his greatest teacher during this period of time. I think that what is implied by this is that it gave him an opportunity to really understand the Western mind deeply. There were so many different groups of people he worked with: teachers, engineers, construction people, business people, psychologists, sociologists, and others. He was able to work with them all. He worked with their motivations, with what they cared about. He has been a tremendous teacher to basically help us transform negativities and strengthen our positivity so we can train ourselves to really accomplish something of value. Work is really the testing ground for him, and he has really made work the key part of our training. Work is something not to be shirked or to think of as a marginal part of our lives and then we'll take a vacation or we'll take a nice weekend somewhere. But to have the actual process of work be very important to us and satisfactory.

I came across a recent survey that suggested that 80 percent of Americans were unhappy in their work. Why do you think this is?

Eighty percent is an astounding number. I think people consider work something that they *have* to do, or that they are doing for material values, something that is going to allow them to do something else. Sort of an external approach to work. I think this takes a little bit of reorienting. If we basically think we can be cheerful, helpful, cooperative, and accomplish something with our work, that's quite a challenge. Most people may not be challenged initially in their work, or they may think they have certain limits. Their mind has certain limits with it. But perhaps a better way of looking at that is, asking: Why do people work? It is quite an interesting question. Why are we here? What are we doing?

Usually if you ask that question, after a little bit, a couple things usually come up. First, people want to be happy. They want to feel happy in what they are doing. Second, they want to accomplish something of value. And third, they want to do something that they feel is balanced and healthy. Those are usually the deeper reasons. People may need to ask themselves a question: Why am I doing this? Is this so I can do these type of things? Am I happy with this? And this isn't just people who work, by the way. You could take this to the spiritual communities as well. You could ask the same question.

When I was growing up (and I think in some ways this has continued), somehow work was compartmentalized from one's life. You had your life and you had your work. My parents had their life and they had their work. Work was something external. It was something out there that you did in order to live your life, in order to keep a roof over your head. I remember going to a career counselor when I was in high school. They were taking the results of college boards or SAT tests or whatever. Well, this is what it looks like you should do. You should train for this career, as if you only had one career in your entire life. I think I've had about six since school, and maybe even more if I think about it. There is something about the compartmentalization of work, the separating. From what I've gleaned from these workshops that you are doing and the book itself, there's not a separation. It's like really bringing your life together with whatever it is you are doing in the world called work. And it's also bringing in the inner with the outer—the inner being our innermost spiritual drives with our outer expression. Is that right?

Yes, very much so. Work basically becomes an expression and also an unusual opportunity. By opportunity, I mean certainly we all have strengths and weaknesses. It gives us a chance to reflect on this and to see where we are weak and what type of results we are getting.

I would think that the conditioning we have that has us see work in a certain way is something that we have to really get in touch with and overcome. Is that not true?

Yes, I think really what we are talking about is that we have to retrain our mind and encourage and nourish our mind so we begin to see that every moment doesn't make any difference where we are. This type of awareness or concentration or energy, this being alive, fully engaging in life, that's what we really want to train to do. If we separate or compartmentalize, usually we hold something back. We don't really engage in it fully. I think of Thoreau's statement, that, "Most men lead lives of quiet desperation." They are not really engaged in it. Or to put it in another way: We treat work as part of our day, and then we end up living in the margins of life.

Thoreau also said, "Any job that requires new clothes, don't take it." He had a lot of things to say about work, that's for sure.

Now is an opportunity for us to treat work as a challenge where we can really develop our skills. One of the reasons we want to do this as we begin to develop our skills and we become more aware, we become more concentrated, our energy picks up. When our energy and our concentration and awareness start to work well together, we become very creative, very innovative, and very much involved in what we are doing. We become alive. And we've all had that experience. We've all had what some people call "Peak Experiences." We work long hours on a project we are really involved in, or a group of us gets together on a project, and we find that we go beyond 9:00 P.M. stopping, 6:00 A.M. stopping, until we really finish it. And after that, we feel filled with a joy and satisfaction that we completed this. Full of energy—actually more energy than when we began. You start to realize there's tremendous satisfaction, meaning, and value in work. You can't have a better school than work. It shows the results immediately.

What about time and work? We live in a pace where there is never enough time to do it, never enough time to quite get it finished. What about that?

Time is a very interesting topic. As we are concerned with our work, time and awareness are very much tied together. I can tell you, if you ask a group of people, Give me the reasons you can't become more fully involved in your work, why aren't you really involved in your work, usually the top three reasons are: One, I don't have enough money to do whatever I want to do. I don't have enough time. And usually something like, I have a cat or dog to take care of. Something minor like that. Time is always the quotient that comes out. And when we look carefully, we recognize that we waste lots of time. This is where training ourselves in how to use time is very important to what we do. The closer you are tied with time, the less you fight time.

As soon as you start fighting time, you find yourself in a battle. Things don't go well. We're not connected very well. But when we are able to get in flow with time, things go quite well and quite quickly. So, I think we all say we don't have enough time. You never really hear a problem about, "I don't have the space to practice in my house or to make a work table," or whatever. No one complains about space, but time—everyone sort of winces. They say, Oh, I don't know. I have all these other responsibilities. So, the way to really utilize our time is to be able to train our mind and time together. When these two go together, it is really quite interesting what can happen.

As you say, getting in touch with the flow of time—that sounds a lot easier than it may be. What does one do to approach time? What is a first step or second or third step?

The wonderful thing about this book *Mastering Successful Work*, is there are many exercises. We have lots of exercises on time. The purpose of the exercises on time is so we really begin to see how our time is used. If we are not aware of how we use time, then it is very difficult. And for the most part, unless we are very careful observers, we don't see how we waste five minutes going to the coffee pot, and we don't see how we waste ten minutes talking with the neighbor, or we don't see how we walk down the hall, and before we know it we forget what we went down the hall for.

So you have to really begin to train the mind. And we have a few exercises. One is really a daily checklist that is very, very helpful in getting in touch with time. The exercise is quite simple in one way. It really doesn't ask too much of you. At the beginning of the day, you can say, What do I want to accomplish today? Then you say, Let me go through this particular list, and then you go back at the end of the day, and say, How well did I do?

For example: *What are my priorities for this day?* So you really take a good look and sort of sort through. Okay, today these are my priorities. Then you ask yourself, a very important question: *How will I focus my awareness?* In other words, how will you look at all aspects of these priorities? Not just one direction. But look around. And the third thing I think is probably the most interesting and that is: *How will I measure my success?* I think this is probably the thing we have found on our retreats that is the most interesting development for people when they start measuring their success. We often have very simple tasks of mailings or making cards or gardening or sort of repetitious-type work. Usually most people are not used to repetitive-type work. We don't seem to attract that type of people. So assuming we have a large mailing to go out, we keep a count, every hour, how many we do. The first two weeks, people object to measuring how much they do of anything. I think we all do. We resent this. We don't want this type of accurate feedback. One day we may do 50, the next day we may do 100, the next day we may do 60.

Then after about two weeks, you begin to realize that quite a bit of the variance is really on really concentrating, really being aware of what we are doing. And then it becomes a challenge as you begin to realize you sort of space out or take a vacation. Then as the mind begins to concentrate, the awareness begins to pick up. You see people who are very appreciative of this ability to have the time to watch and measure how they do. The measuring of the success is very interesting. There are occupations where people say, Oh, I can't really measure it. But when they do measure it, they feel okay—now I can see what's going on. At first there is a little bit of resistance to measuring, and then there's great appreciation that we can really see with awareness how our mind is working so we can able to focus it.

Then the next question we usually ask is: *Who is depending on me for that day?* And this has a lot of different ramifications. It may just mean someone who is depending on you to meet them for lunch so they can discuss what they want, and also from our side, who's depending on me? Children, parents, the whole thing. And then the interesting question: *What am I forgetting or ignoring?* And if you begin to go through this checklist every day for about two weeks, after a while you begin to see that you are starting to use your time better, your priorities, you understand where you are going. I think it is very important, Michael, that at the very bottom of this is the real understanding that each of us has something of value we'd like to accomplish in our life. And if you really feel that way, that indeed there is something I'd like to accomplish; this really helps you get in touch with time to accomplish it.

There is a simple explanation of this that I think is very interesting. If we have only 24 hours a day, which I think we all think is a given, by the time we eat and sleep and take care of our needs, we probably have 12 hours. Then recreation and taking care of other people and television probably takes another four hours. That leaves eight hours. Then we think, Okay, for five minutes to an hour, I'm sort of fantasizing about the future—that's another hour lost and we are down to seven. Then we have illnesses and commuting, and all that probably takes another two hours. This and that takes another hour. You are probably down to four hours of really productive time that you can use for what you want. If you say there is something I want to accomplish, some vision or some goal or purpose, then you realize you have 4 hours available out of 12. Well, that is 25 percent of our capacity. If this were a physical realm rather than a mental realm, we'd say we were severely handicapped, as we are only using 25 percent of our capacity. So if you begin to focus on something you think is of value, something you want to create, you recognize that you have to make time an ally.

We only have so much time. If we only have another four years left, it means we only have ten hours of real productive time to get done what we want to get done. So, by focusing time and disciplining the mind, you begin to concentrate. The awareness begins to pick up. Our energy begins to pick up. We become more and more creative, and certainly more and more productive.

I think we often become unconscious of how we spend our time. Just by realizing if we got up an hour earlier every day, and you start to compute that out, it actually works out to something like adding two weeks to a year. Two weeks that you slept that you could apply to something else that you want to do. There was a book that came out a few years ago called Your Money or Your Life, *based on a series of workshops that a man named Joe Dominguez gave around the country, helping people to get in touch with money and how we use money. The way he did that was by getting people in touch with time—how time is equivalent to money, and money is equivalent to how much time you put in to make it. If you spend $25, how much time did you spend to gener-ate that $25? And you start to get this equation of where your time is going. And your time's going to make money. And if your lifestyle requires more money, that means more time, et cetera. You really get in touch with the time aspect, particularly as it relates to*

generating money, to generating material goods, or whatever it is
you are spending money for.

As you become more and more involved with time, one of the great thrills is when you can actually expand time. There is a little exercise, like to give 5 percent more effort to what you are doing. That extra 5 percent is incredible, absolutely unbelievable. You can clean your desk, those phone calls you've been wanting to put off—you make the phone calls—all of a sudden the mind becomes clear, the desk becomes clear, all these little hold backs that sort of accumulate under the rug until we trip over them. Just a little bit, five or ten minutes or an hour a day is very helpful.

I think everybody is interested in expanding time.

This is something we've found, first of all, that picks up your energy. Second of all, you feel enormous satisfaction from it. You just have this feeling of well-being from the whole exercise. It sounds a little difficult at first, but it is not that difficult. What you do is you take every hour, or if you like, two hours, and set a dead-line for what you want to accomplish. So you list your six things you want to accomplish in this hour or these two hours. Then at the end of that, you look back and say, All right, how did I do? If you did all of it, wonderful. Set some more for the next two-hour period. If there are some you haven't been able to quite finish, you just put it into the next period. And very importantly, don't blame yourself. Don't get into guilt or feel fearful that you didn't finish it. Just sort of look from a neutral position and say, Okay, I'll finish it the next time.

So after the first day of eight hours working with this, you are quite surprised by how much you accomplish. By the time the second day goes by, you are astonished. All these things you've had in corners are now cleaned up. The desk is clean, the floor is swept, and all of a sudden, you sort of have this eager, "What else?

What else can I do?" You realize that you are starting to operate at greater capability. So you have a knowledge coming up from this process that is just wonderful. Then, the third day, it continues. Maybe late in the third or fourth day, you stop. And this is normal. Almost everyone stops. And the question is: Why do we stop? I'm feeling better. I'm getting a lot done. I'm ready to tackle more things. Why do we stop?

At that point, it is very, very important just to look and see what story we told ourselves. What story did our mind come up with once again to sidetrack us? Oh, this isn't so difficult. I did this. It's something that anyone can do. Okay, now what? All these little stories. It's very important to pause and say, Okay, I really didn't want to stop, but I did. What was the reason? You look very objectively and quietly. Oh, this was the reason. And then start again. And you'll begin to see very quickly what kind of tricks the mind plays that stop you from really working at your capacity. This type of awareness and concentration working together—after a week or so, it makes a big difference.

I have done that myself, actually, and I always amaze myself. Whenever I do this, whenever I say, Okay, I've got these six things to do and three-and-a-half hours to do them, somehow they always get done. Why don't I do that all the time? It's true, you fall back into another pattern, an old pattern. You have to keep reminding yourself.

I've had the good fortune to be with people who are amazing accomplishers. They attain a lot. I think of Joe Campbell. Joe was someone whose life was dedicated to the world of mythology, so he became the world's greatest popularizer of mythology during his lifetime. He used to tell a story about someone coming up to him and asking him how could he possibly have written so many books. And his answer was, Well, I've spent 40 years doing nothing but writing 12 hours a day. Such a great answer, because that's what it takes. It takes that kind of focus, dedication, and commitment to get it done. Somewhere I think we've all got some piece that was put in there, programmed into us, that said there was something easy about it. Once you got on your track, it was going to be easy. Buy more "how to" books. We're always looking for the magic three steps, the magic ten answers. How to do it quickly. And it doesn't exist, really. It only exists in our capacity to commit. Is that true? Do you think that's true?

I think *commit* is an interesting word. Really, to make a commitment to use our capabilities is extraordinary. Most of us don't really invite responsibility and discipline into our lives. We really think we would prefer the easy way—you know, procrastination and our own laziness and forgetfulness. The question of really using our capabilities and inviting more responsibility into our life—usually people don't want to do that. They don't really want to be that committed to life, to really using their time well. So I think you've hit a big subject. I think it all will get back to how we encourage, how we educate, how we nourish our mind, so we can penetrate these kind of obstacles, of thinking things are easy, thinking that someone else will do it for me. Basically, building our own confidence in our abilities and in our own knowledge—this is really what skillful means.

I think that the commitment issue is an important one. My partner, Justine, and I, we have this little repartee about, Well, what is your level for commitment in that one? And years ago I took a seminar. It was a six-day seminar mostly for corporate CEOs, and somehow I got invited to do it. One of the things they talked about there was commitment, and they had levels of commitment. A plus-two commitment might be: It's a great idea, let's do it. There's a level of commitment there, but then you move up to another level. The top level of commitment is: Yeah, it's as good as done, no matter what. So that's the level of commitment that one wants to get to, that I want to get to, and operate as much as I pos-

sibly can at that level of commitment. Any level less than that, it doesn't quite get done in the same way. It's really important to look at what commitment is really about.

I think this is true, and I think you may think about it from a different point of view if you replace the word *commitment* with *caring.* If you have that kind of caring, that when you say, "It will be done," you know that you care enough that it will be followed through; it will be taken care of. It doesn't say that we won't make mistakes. We all make mistakes. We'll learn from the mistakes, but we'll still continue to take care of this. This is really what fully engaging is. The heart, the mind are fully engaged this type of care that we will be that responsible, to make this happen, to accomplish what we set out to do. It's very important. It starts with very small steps, small tasks, and then it continues to build. And when it starts to build, the momentum gets very large. We take on many projects, many ideas we never dreamed we'd be involved in. And here we find ourselves fully involved in making these happen.

We have another saying around New Dimensions: "Our goal is perfection, and we'll settle for excellence." We are all addicts to perfection. We Americans seem to grow up with this.

This isn't only American, I can tell you, because when we give retreats, as I said, they are all international. I'd say the first problem that really comes up, particularly when we shorten the length of time and increase the volume of what we want, which always puts a certain urgency of time to a task, is the question of quality versus quantity. Every culture has this. And those with a strong perfectionist nature fight with those who want more production. And this balance, getting into the flow of this, or getting out of the way and really falling into the flow, is a very interesting dynamic of mastering successful work.

How does one integrate one's spiritual practice into one's work?

It starts with training the mind. As our awareness starts to pick up, we naturally become more sensitive. It's a wonderful tool, the mind. When we can really concentrate with our awareness, we concentrate exactly on what we are doing, and we can accomplish it. Many of the negative internal dialogues such as "I can't do it," "I don't know enough," "I don't have enough," "I'm not educated enough," "I don't have enough materials," "There's someone else who knows more," "The technology is not right"—these little voices grow quiet as we concentrate on actually doing the task. This is quite a development. When you are really able to concentrate that mind, we don't undermine our own success. Most of the time it's ourselves, the internal dialogue that undermines us. It's not anyone we can blame. What I can tell you is that no matter where you are in the world, if you have success, most people take the success as their own; if you have failure, then the blame starts. It's not my failure. Workers blame the boss, the boss blames the workers, the workers blame the manager, and it continues around. And wherever you are in the world, everyone blames the economy.

And if you are an American, everybody blames the president or Congress. They are useful whipping dogs.

Exactly. It's anything but really looking. But when we look clearly at our own minds, if we can change this type of thing, if we can really look directly at our mistakes and at our opportunities, then we are able to focus the mind and move ahead. Also, I think it's important to speak a little bit about energy, because when the mind and your heart are really focusing on something, your energy picks up. It's difficult sometimes, when your energy is low, to get yourself out of that doldrum state of mind. So the energy picking up really works well. Mastering successful work has to do with increasing our awareness and focusing our concentration and increasing the energy. When these three all work together, we become very much alive, very much engaged in life—quite often spontaneous and joyful.

Whenever you are with someone who has this capacity or exercises the principles you are talking about, it is very compelling. One is magnetically attracted to that kind of energy. I think that is one of the keys. Anyone who is able to move in the practice you are talking about—it's like attracting energy. People are drawn to that energy. So the usual excuse that one hears a lot is, "I can't do what I really want to do because I don't have enough money." That's a common one. Do you hear that a lot?

That's the number-one excuse. The next is: "I don't have enough time."

So what's the answer to "I don't have enough money"?

First of all, we have to look at a little different view of it because it's difficult to immediately say, Well, you *do* have enough money. That's not the issue. The issue really is how the mind continues to tell us the same stories. So we buy it, as in "I don't have enough money." We quit on something our heart really might want. "I don't have enough time" is the same story. So what we begin to see after a period of time is that the mind continues to come up with the same excuses, and each time we dutifully obey. We submit to the stories of the mind. Then we can see other people who had far less, and they do exactly what we wanted to do. It never really bothered them. So we have to really look and see how we penetrate our stories. This is really the art of skillful means. These internal obstacles that say, "I don't have enough time or money." What you would call "the shortage" or "the limitations" or the victim-type mentality. "I don't have enough of this," "I don't have enough time"—it's all under a category of sort of a hopeless way of being. Work, then, becomes sheer frustration. This really is a deeply painful experience.

If one doesn't have the experience of hanging out there in space without the usual kind of security blankets that we tend to attach ourselves to—like, a salary, job, insurance, a car, et cetera—whatever it is that we attach ourselves to for security— that can be very scary for someone to think of jumping into a space that doesn't have any of those things, those things that we are used to attaching ourselves to for security.

It's unknown territory.

And it's very scary. So how does one make that leap and jump into the abyss, as it were, of letting go of all those, because I am committed to doing what I want to do, and I'm going to do it no matter what?

You've hit fear. Fear is certainly one of the reasons we buy into it. We make a great case for our fear. This may be quite an assumption that is challengeable. First of all, we can challenge it. Second of all, often we learn by doing. Okay? The only way we really learn is to get in there and do it, to take some action; otherwise, we are sort of cathartic, we can't move, we're just stuck. Our fears have gotten so large that we can't take effect. So the first solution is: Take a small step. Take some action. Then, after you take a small action, another one—baby steps, but they go a long way. If we think that after the first step we are going to jump over the mountain, I think that is a big mistake.

That's another salient point, too. Many of us are conditioned to that idea that having a vision, seeing a goal, that somehow, if we take a few steps, we are going to achieve the vision, we are going to achieve the goal. Sort of like going from A to Z without passing through BCDEF. It's like going from the beginning to the end without any of the in-between. It doesn't work that way.

No, the first obstacle comes up and you give up. So you have to have the determination and the effort to work through obstacles. Because, for sure, they are going to come up. I would say that if people have the vision and the commitment and the goal, they are fortunate. Then they just need determination to really bring up their awareness and their energy and their concentration, and it's beyond what we believe we can achieve. The mind, once it starts to break through the limits—is quite a freeing experience to realize what we are really capable of. It's a marvelous thing to see creativity occur, and you really never know how it's going to come up, but quite often the only way to do it is to learn by doing. You have to act.

Isn't one of the questions that is useful to ask: "What is the purpose of my work—whatever it is I am doing now?" Isn't that a useful question?

Sure. How we attach ourselves to the value of what we are doing is very important. There are a couple of questions that really tie the vision to deeper questions that I think are quite helpful to keep in mind. These questions broaden our perspective. One of those might be: "How can I help?" And another may be: "What are my deepest purposes?" Many people would like this last question to be something we think about often or have thought about in the past. Sometimes we ignore: "What do I wish to contribute to the world?" I think those questions can quite often tie you very much into a good perspective of where you are going. And if we are fortunate to have a good focus and we use our time well, we can usually accomplish what we want.

What about negativity? The idea of comparison, that kind of, "Well, I'm not doing it as good as the next person, or that other company." There is a negativity that kinds of creeps around. What about that?

Negativity is certainly something. We even teach workshops on combating negativity now because you've hit such a big topic. Again, these questions of competitiveness, someone doing better, jealousy, envy—this type of thing that doesn't let us rest and enjoy or appreciate our own accomplishments is something that can be easily combated. So, turning to the positive, you may need exercises to help turn to the positive, or you may need the ability to not pay attention to that type of voice. This is where those voices don't occur. Then we break the concentration, or we see something that may occur when we're vague or we are not as well concentrated. So I think as we begin to really concentrate the mind, and our awareness picks up, these don't bother us as much as they once did. But it isn't to say they don't occur. It isn't to say that life is just a bed of roses. These do occur. Sometimes they can actually throw us off from what we are doing, but as we continue to work hard and really concentrate on the mind, they don't seem to last as long, and eventually they don't have the same bite; they don't really bite into us or cause us so much pain anymore.

Sometimes when you pursue such a track, it sometimes seems very unusual or different to the people who have been part of your community or part of your milieu or family or whatever. You know, when you leave work you've been involved in for 20 years or whatever, and go off to do something else, it may look strange to somebody else. You may say, "Well, I don't have a job, but I'm just going to do this. They say, "Well, you can't do that." There's a rampant cynicism afoot in our society. It is present everywhere. And then there's a kind of negativity, particularly from people who haven't done it. They are always willing to say, "You can't." There aren't too many people who are saying that you can.

We call that a conspiracy. This is sort of a conspiracy of our friends, or a conspiracy of those people we work with. We all conspire together so we don't go out and do these things. It's almost like when you see these tanks with lobster or crabs, one starts to climb up over the edge of it, and all of a sudden, another crab grabs it and pulls it back down. This type of thing is very frightening for people because our friends may change or we may actually move locations. We may feel very lonely. But I think this is where we begin to trust ourselves, where this real confidence starts to come out—knowing that we can accomplish what we want.

I love your expression, "I can." I think it's very seldom that you look in your office or your relationships or you ask someone to do something, and they say, "I can do it," and it's done. You don't think twice about it. Most people you ask, there's an excuse. "Well, can I do it later? Can you send it down the hall? Can someone else do it?" There's all this inbred negativity. Now we may not recognize it at the time as negativity, but when you see someone who says, "I can. I'll take care of it," you have this uplifting of the heart and the spirit immediately, that something so positive can happen. It's these levels that can be quite subtle, Michael. How deep this negativity goes. It is our resistance to change. We are really talking about change. We are really trying to transform ourselves out of this particular habit pattern we have that we may even see as destructive. If we don't see it as destructive, we can see that it is holding us back from really using our full potential.

It is as simple as seeing the glass half full or half empty.

Initially it may be that, but you are counting on it to be filled by that person. If you ask them to fill the glass, and they say, "I can," and they do fill the glass, then you're really talking about action and results. Then you can measure it. In other words, one of the things you often hear is that the business point of view, the bottom-line point of view, is too result or action oriented. And while it may have its drawbacks, one of the wonderful things about it is you can actually have results and see and measure it. You can see if it's succeeding, if it's going well or if it's not going well, and you can make adjustments accordingly. But it's a very positive thing when someone says, "Not only do I see the glass half filled, but if you'd like it full, I'll fill it for you."

I think there's a level of responsibility that is present in that situation, a level of commitment, a level of inner trust and acceptance. A lot of things have to be present for that to happen.

There are a lot of things present, and this is why this is so important. This is why the techniques aren't necessarily: "Do these five things like we described before." This isn't just these five things. They are sort of temporal. But these work with something a little bit deeper. Really changing our views, how we treat challenges. There is a very interesting quote: "The first step in taking on greater responsibility is to motivate ourselves to positively respond to challenge." That is an interesting idea—to motivate ourselves positively if we are challenged. If someone comes in and gives us more than we think we can do, we have our particular set limits. We only have so much, and then you can fill in the blank. If someone really gives you a challenge, your heart responds and says, "I'd like to try that; I'd like to bite my teeth into that." And within a very brief period of time, your reasons come up: "Oh, I really can't do that. It's not really suited. I'm not educated. I might fail. I'd be embarrassed. I may succeed." Some people don't want to succeed. And there we are caught again in the same little tight loop. We are not able to expand. It is an interesting idea to continue to expand and not constrict, a very interesting idea.

EPILOGUE

By asking new questions about what we are doing and why it can take us more deeply into living a more meaningful life, and by letting work guide us toward inner knowledge, we can live each day with a sense of enjoyment and a feeling that we have accomplished something of worth. When we combine the practical aspects of earning a living with the insights that emerge in spiritual practice, life becomes more joyful and we achieve better results. Work can become a pathway to knowledge rich in satisfaction and accomplishment. The opportunity is here and now. The ultimate responsibility is our own destiny—to wake up and fulfill our own destiny.

CHAPTER NINE

Natural Creativity for Organizations

Margaret Wheatley, Myron Kellner-Rogers,
and Michael Toms

PROLOGUE

*T*here is a simpler way to organize human endeavor. It requires
a new way of being in the world. It requires being in the world
without fear, being in the world with play and creativity, seeking
what's possible, being willing to learn and to be surprised. This
simpler way to organize human endeavor requires a belief that the
world is inherently orderly. The world seeks organization; it does
not need us humans to organize it. This simpler way summons
forth what is best about us. It asks us to understand human nature
differently, more optimistically. It identifies us as creative. It
acknowledges that we seek meaning. It asks us to be less serious,
yet more purposeful about our work and our lives. It does not separate play from the nature of being. In this world, we can move

with more assurance. The world supports our efforts more than we could have hoped. We can create, experiment, organize, fail, accomplish, play, learn, and create again.

These are the words of Margaret Wheatley and Myron Kellner-Rogers. Margaret Wheatley is president of the Berkana Institute and a principal of Kellner-Rogers and Wheatley, Incorporated. She was formerly associate professor of management at the Marriott School of Management, Brigham Young University. For the past several years, she's been working with organizations that want to achieve organizational coherence in the midst of chaotic environments. Her book, Leadership in the New Science: Learning about Organization from an Orderly Universe, *was named the best management book of 1992 by* Industry Week.

Myron Kellner-Rogers is a principal of Kellner-Rogers and Wheatley and a founder and trustee of the Berkana Institute. With two decades of experience, both as consultant and executive, Myron's work now focuses on applying insight from the new sciences of chaos, complexity, and self-organizing systems to assisting organizations in coping with turbulent environments. Both Meg and Myron are frequent keynote speakers in the US and abroad. They're the co-authors of A Simpler Way, *which discusses the new self-organizing paradigm for organizations*

MICHAEL TOMS: *What does play have to do with organization?*

MARGARET WHEATLEY: It's really just to think about what play has to do with life and why in our organizational lives we've made it so foreign to our experience. I mean, everywhere you look in life, what you see is enormous creativity and enormous diversity and experimentation. Then you take that into our organizations, and instead, what you see is little tiny boxes, great levels of fear, and then we come in with training programs to kind of reinstitute this creativity that is only supposed to be possessed by a very small percentage of the people.

Within that play aspect of being in an organization, being in work, you also talk about the freedom to fail. That's something. We're always worried about making mistakes. You know, get it right the first time. That kind of attitude. What about that?

MYRON KELLNER-ROGERS: I have a four-year-old son who is a master of play. He knows how to play incredibly well. I've spent long hours just watching what he does. In trying to understand it, what I sense is an overwhelming presence totally connected in the mind. Beginning to play with something that's in front of him, it becomes an object that isn't what its intended purpose is; it creates a whole life. Then something that wasn't in his perception suddenly appears, and he'll reach for it, it'll come in, it'll be incorporated. He'll try to do something with it; it won't work, it'll be discarded, he'll move on to the next thing. That kind of flow and freedom that happens in truly creative play—that's certainly lost in our organizations. The kind of inventiveness that can happen requires us to be able to fail in the true sense of the word—to be able to fail and to walk away from that failure and to learn from it. The learning that is embodied in failure, especially with a child and certainly in our organizations, is overwhelming. We're missing it.

MARGARET: If you look at our lives and organizations, we fail all the time, but instead of being in a system that says how can we learn from this, we have to scurry like crazy to cover up the fact that we just made a mistake. We had worked with one client from a major global manufacturing company who said that they had a phrase there, which was that prudent risks were acceptable. He said after many years there, I realized a prudent risk was one that had succeeded. He changed the language in his own organization. He said, here we do experiments and they were chemical manufacturing so it made sense to them. But it's a very nice switch. I mean, if we're experimenting, we're experimenting to learn what works and what doesn't work. Then the idea of risk is a very different issue. Risk is related to our fear of failing.

MYRON: In any experiment, there is no failure. The results are the results, and they're instructive.

Do you think that aspect of fear, feeling afraid to make mistakes, is rooted in our educational system? The way we're taught and educated that if we make mistakes, we fail. You know, we get F's on tests, we don't do it right. The whole attitude toward having to do it perfectly. How do we go past thinking that there is only one right answer?

MARGARET: There is so much good thinking being done in public education, but it's one of the great institutions that's in total disarray, like all of them. The desire to stop rewarding students for performance on standardized tests and move toward portfolios, which is an expression of their individuality, is something very significant. We have to go deeply into our educational system, but we're meeting an awful lot of educators who are already in that question and who are experimenting.

MYRON: To go past that sense of failure of getting the right answer, we need to go back to what has created that dominance in our society for getting it right the first time, and it's everywhere around us. Certainly, the trend with a mechanistic worldview that is now beginning to give way to something different in our book and in all our work—we're talking about a living systems perspective about how life organizes itself. That includes the ability to fail and actually requires great failure and tinkering and playing with the environment in order to find right answers. You know, schools are no different than our corporate industrial organizations or other bureaucracies. They model a dominant way of thinking about what is the best way to organize human endeavor. That way has been as a machine. What we call into question is whether or not human beings can operate effectively and well as machines.

Do you think life supports risk taking?

MARGARET: Well, life clearly supports experimentation. One Catholic theologian, I think it was David Stindell-Rast, said that if you want to understand creativity and experimentation, just look at a tree and see how many birds there are. I mean, there isn't one bird. The Creator didn't survey it, benchmark it, and come up with the ideal bird and now that's all you see. The diversity of life is shocking, I think, even to scientists in our day and age. We just had no sense of the range of expression that life was revealing to us until quite recently. It's a humbling moment in biology as we're trying to categorize even what we're discovering in these diverse forms.

I don't want anyone to think that we're proposing something new, like take a risk or be free to fail. What's interesting is that if we were truthful about our own experiences and organizations, we would fail all the time. We're just not in a culture that allows us to talk about it or to learn from it. Then we come in from another way and say, Well, we've got to start learning from experiences, but that becomes a very structured program rather than just figuring out how can we be in a conversation to support one another's learning. I mean, that's what the failure of conversation is about. Nothing will work right the first time. It's not my life experience, and I doubt it's any reader's experience. So how do we get into this crazy expectation that you must do it right the first time and if you don't, you're not going to talk about it? How did we get so disoriented from how to learn and create together? I find this very puzzling.

Do you have any answers to that question that you just posed? How do we get there? How did we get here?

MARGARET: How did we get here? We have a huge mirage in our thinking that we could treat people with machine efficiencies. Machines have no intelligence of their own. You don't expect them to create it; they just follow instructions. So they bear no resemblance to human beings whatsoever. Yet we have a culture that over the past several hundred years and increasingly in our large organizations in the past five years or so that has said that human beings are better treated as machines. So give a person a set of directions, expect them to follow it. Now if anyone really follows directions from another human being, I haven't met them. I'd be intrigued to meet that person. People are always exerting their independence and their creativity. Well, why on earth wouldn't we try and marshal that in an organizational setting—whether it's a community organization or a large global corporation?

The way we've set it up, independence and creativity are problems for us because what we want is control and a machine sense of efficiency that has nothing to do with the way life actually is. So a lot of it for us is this belief that the world is best understood as a machine, and human beings are best understood as machines.

What happens to planning and goals and objectives and that kind of scenario where you're kind of allowing everybody to be whatever they want to be? What do you do about plans? Can you really plan at all in that kind of context?

MYRON: The notion used to be that a strategically planned organization could look five years out and plan what it is going to do, how to do it, and what path to take to get there. I think, happily, most people are no longer diluted by the ability to do it in that step-by-step, moment-to-moment fashion. Some people talk about the kind of intuitive decision-making process that they've been engaged in and then do some retrospective rationale. About five years from now, if we're in a place that we like, we will point back and say remember five years ago when we set the plan to get here. It's kind of a re-creation of history. Most of us tell ourselves that it was predictable, controllable, and measurable as we moved along this particular path.

What about such things as five-year plans?

MARGARET: They're a well-endangered species.

MYRON: What we're talking about is replacing an exercise that wasn't doing anybody much good and required an awful lot of energy from an organization. Everything from all the exercises that we went through from senior levels to departmental levels in any organization, including communities who run themselves this way. Constructing the plan, developing the measures, watching for the measurement of the plan over time. At the end of the year, evaluating each person as far as how well we did on our portion of the plan. That's being replaced, I believe, with trying to seek a way for the intelligence of the organization to be connected to its environment in the moment of what's required from us.

As an individual, my sense of where I'm going is that I don't have a five-year plan for myself, I'm sorry to say. If I did, I know I'd fail in getting there. That might be one of the reasons I let it go. My sense of myself is that as each new situation arises, I am using my intelligence, my spirit, any of the forces that I have available to me rooted in my identity to respond to my environment and to become more of who it is I want to become in my life. The organization's ability to move in a path of becoming more of what it chooses to be and what people are capable of requires a different kind of sensitivity that isn't so much setting the future and trying to achieve it, as much as it is being in the present and having the desire to go forward.

MARGARET: Our desire to move forward must include a clear intent and a growing understanding of who we are, what we're good at, and what we're not so good at—there's an important notion of intentionality here, just as we were talking about that at the personal level. Organizations don't just wander aimlessly, although we see a lot of those, by the way. They end up in businesses that are disastrous to them, and then they sell them off and they wander someplace else. To have an intentionality about what we think is our focus. What we think is our expertise, and then to engage the organization and to be much more alert and acute sensors of what opportunities suddenly appear—that's the shift we're talking about. It's how do you think all the time and be much more conscious, rather than put all of this time, money, and people into planning sessions that end up in nicely bound documents that no one references after they're created.

How would you define intentionality *or* intention?

MARGARET: I think it includes a clear sense of what we're good at, this notion of the competencies of an organization, the people in it, and what the organization is particularly skilled at. It includes what we've learned from our different efforts, if we've tried different businesses. Sometimes we sum this up as emotionally as we can with organizations, and why is the world different because we've got to work together? What is it that we want to create together that wasn't possible in any other organizations? Then, why would the world even notice that we existed? It may be that we're going to be the premier manufacturer of miniaturized refrigerators or something, but at least we've had a deep conversation about the why of working together.

We find when those conversations happen, and they continually happen, that people engaged feel welcomed to be engaged in their work with their own deep sense of purpose. The energy and commitment that comes forth is unlike anything that's available in these very bland statements such as, Well, here's our mission statement. Put it on your wall so you'll know where it is. You know, we've taken these deeply emotive forces, like connecting purpose, my purpose to the organization's purpose. Or trying to inspire what is a naturally occurring desire to make your life mean something. We've taken that and just removed it from our lives together in organizations. Then we wonder why people aren't committed, why people are burnt out, why people don't want to work together.

One of the things that you took on in A Simpler Way *was evolution and Darwin's notion of the survival of the fittest. Can you talk a little bit about that?*

MARGARET: Two of the scientists whom we've learned a lot from are Humberto Maturana and Francisco Varela, and they had a wonderful way of expressing this. They said it is not survival of the fittest; it's not that strongly competitive. It's not that desperation to figure out how you'll be the lone survivor. It's not survival of the fittest; it's survival of the fit. Varela, who gets quite poetic in his scientific expressions, said many paths of change are possible. But it's a path of continuous tinkering. What we love about that lens of this approach to evolution is that the world is a lot friendlier and less hostile and more cooperative for many forms, for much more diversity than the Darwinian view has led us to believe. In our newer understandings of the planet, we realize that life has been here since the beginning. It wasn't an accident. It didn't just show up and then have to fight for survival constantly. Now people do feel in their organizations often that they have to fight for survival constantly, but that's not how it is once you step outside these buildings and get into the natural world. It's a very system-seeking, highly symbiotic partnering relationship that characterizes the way life develops itself.

It certainly has come out of the Darwinian view that evolution is a struggle, probably translating also as life is a struggle. You have a different view?

MYRON: Struggle gets translated in our relationships with one another as get it right or die. Our notion of the natural world is that if a species doesn't make it, it's because it was stupid. Somebody we work with who is in a gas business talks about living off the dinosaurs. He asked this question: How long were the dinosaurs on earth? And it's 65 million years or whatever, and that always shocks people because we've developed this thing that they got it wrong and they disappeared. In our organizations, how that translates, if we go back to what we were talking about earlier—about experimenting and play and risk taking—it really works counter to that because it says that if we don't find the right answer and implement it correctly the first time, we're not going to be around here next year, or I personally am not going to be around here next year. It puts something into our relationships that not only has organizations competing against organizations in a survival-of-the-fittest way. It also has me as an individual competing against you. If we go through the kind of repercussions of the current spate of downsizing in the last couple of years in the United States, at least in other places, what has done to color, to heighten that sense of, it's my survival against your survival. It's working very much against what we know to be forces that support all life on this planet. We're working counter to them somehow, in our relationships with one another.

Let's take that for a moment and apply it to the world of capitalism and business, where competition is fierce. Would you see that changing in the context of the worldview that you're espousing?

MARGARET: It is already changing. In many ways, I think what we're describing is a world that exists, but that we haven't had the desire or the language to look at it. Now we are, in very capitalistic terms, starting to notice that alliances, partnering, sharing of information—that those things make a difference to our overall health and that a whole industry like silicon-chip manufacturing actually thrives on a very different model of both collaboration and competition. But there's an awful lot of competition that people never expected in their old beliefs about ruthless competition. It just frustrates me that we haven't been willing to look at our experience and see what else we might be learning. We've really been blindsided by this notion that business must be competitive because nature is competitive and only the strong survive. A biologist, whom we love, Lynn Margulis, who is also one of the proponents of the Gaia hypothesis with James Lovelock, talks about the earth as an organism that can sustain itself and create the conditions for more life. She just looks at the evolutionary record and says that brutal species come and go, but they don't survive. It's only cooperation that increases over time, if you look at the record of life.

Another interesting fact that you brought out from the biophysical history of the planet was the appearance of oxygen. Maybe you can tell us that little story.

MARGARET: It's a wonderful example of life's incredible ability to diversify and change and make more life possible. In the early stages of bacteria, they could not survive on oxygen at all, and a holocaust took place because the oxygen increased in the atmosphere. It was just obliterating life. Then the blue-green algae just figured out a way to make the oxygen vital for their survival, and they invented photosynthesis. I think we look at that sort of incredible adaptability—taking something that was a threat and turning it into a partner. We look at that level of the bacteria theory—well, that was a good thing, but when someone in our midst tries to defy our plans for how something should be and shows us their creative solution, we often pull back from it. But the blue-green bacteria are wonderful examples of this kind of adaptability.

It reminded me of the discovery of life forms in the Pacific vents, where the fires are coming at 2,000 degrees Fahrenheit and they found life forms. They found similar life forms in the Atlantic in the vents, where we didn't think life could exist in such an inhospitable environment.

MARGARET: We have not understood life's incredible ability to diversify and expand. James Lovelock said that wherever we look, whatever ancient rocks we find now, we find life within them. So it's a very different understanding of how necessary life has been through the evolution of the planet and how possible life becomes in places that we thought were impossible because of this incredible creativity.

The reality that life wants to happen so powerfully and so strongly and so consistently—how does that apply to the organization?

MYRON: Beyond the wonderful and dramatic and imagination-creating stories about the beginning of the planet, I think each of us actually has this experience within us—no matter what's going on inside your organization that's shutting down my creativity, that's working against me, bringing forth my best. I find ways to do something that's imaginative, that's different, that's innovative in the context of the organization. People do their best because they want to do their best. Their strongest spirit will come forth because they'll find something that matters to them in the organization. I believe, actually, that many people have the experience of wonderful things happening in their organization in spite of every message that they're getting or every structure of policy or procedure.

Life wants to happen so amazingly much of the time—all the time, really. You have more to say about that?

MARGARET: If you think about life wanting to happen, it wants to happen in all forms of life. Let's just talk about human beings for a while. In our lives, we think we're looking for security. We think we look for self-interest, but if any of us looks into our own experience, we see that we're always tinkering. We notice something that needs improving, and we want to contribute. We may remove a pot in our living space, or it may be how we change something in a production line. Most of us keep our eyes out for ways in which we can tinker things into more effectiveness. That seems to be just a natural occurring phenomenon—not just with humans with our consciousness, but in all of life. This belief that life wants to happen, which we see in our own lives, and then we see it all around us in life; we don't see it in our organizations. I would say that the dominant theme in organizations is that control wants to happen. We exchange creativity for control. We exchange the unpredictable surprises. We give that up so that, instead, we can predict minimum contribution. In this sense, we've done a great injustice to people. Then we don't like what they do. We don't like the fact that this organization isn't innovative enough, isn't creative enough. People aren't taking risks, our quality is off, our customers don't like it, then we turn around and think we have to train people into being creative, or we have to train people into quality.

We're giving ourselves an awfully bad reputation as a species these days, believing that things like quality, the desire to learn, the desire to create, are external to us. It's only a good leader and a good trainer who will somehow put that into us. But this is just a complete lack of realization. It's just a complete blankness to the fact that we've created people and organizations that do not welcome people in as living beings.

It's a strange thing to say, but if you look at most organizations, you would never get the impression that people there are alive. You get the impression that what we want is a kind of obedience and predictable performance. That is, if you want creativity, you give up predictability. If you want innovation, then you've got to be willing to be surprised. If you want people to take risks, then you've got to welcome them in as adult contributors. We're trying to play it very safe with one another in our organizations.

Isn't it true in our lives that we want to control things, we want to know that things are going to be safe? We want to know that we're going to have enough money next week or next month. We want to be secure in our homes. These are control issues. I'm wondering how we change it within the organization or within a business if it means that we have to change it at home, too?

MYRON: I think it requires us to think a lot about how we've approached our own lives, our lives in our families, our relationship with ourselves, our relationship to our communities and to all our organizations. The dominant way of thinking about the universe has been a mechanical one, one that says you can get from X to Z by moving through every letter of the alphabet in sequence, and that's the only path that you can take. It makes sense that we impose that on ourselves to some extent. However, I would say that with the right eyes, if we looked at our own lives, we would find a far greater balance between the desire for security and the freedom to just work with whatever is showing up.

If you're a family, you know that with children you cannot predict moment-to-moment outcomes. You take what comes, and you work with what comes. I think as individuals we have a greater sense of that. In organizations we've traded that off. It isn't that we're talking about organizations that have absolutely no sense of control, but where does control come from in my own life? I believe it comes much more from how I create meaning in my life, what's important to me, where my values are, and those live in me as an individual or in my family every moment of the day. In an organization, they are abstract concepts that are outside of me that are impositions from someone else that I haven't participated in creating. So the balance between freedom and control or freedom and predictability in our organizations is very much out of balance. We surrender all our freedom, all our ability to be in life in the moment and to deal with what's coming and to make something wonderful out of it. The great surprise is that that can happen.

We trade all that off for a policy-and-procedure manual that's 300 volumes. Every time an individual in the organization makes a mistake, we make certain that we create a rule that will prevent any other individual from making that mistake again. If you went through those policy manuals in an organizations and sought only the ones that enabled people to do their work, that supported people in doing their work, you might find that out of five thousand pages, five pages actually work that way.

One of the things that you pointed out in A Simpler Way *was that the world seeks diversity, pluralism, and more possibilities, all of which compel us to change. Why is it that we're so resistant to change?*

MARGARET: I don't think we are; I think that's another great blast we're giving to ourselves, again at the species level— not just as individuals. We just think that humans for some reason, unlike the rest of life, don't know how to participate in this continuously changing creative world. What I see, certainly, is that the processes that are being used in a lot of organizations to ask people to change are themselves worthy of being resistant. The processes are wrong. They should be resisted because they're not inclusionary; they ask us to just follow a new set of instructions. They ask us to wait and trust the judgment of our leaders for what's best. They ask us to give up things that are important to us for some corporate justification. But we're not engaging people in the processes of facing the need to change. When we do, the reports that come out of organizations are that people who are engaged in redesigning organizations consistently will redesign themselves out of their jobs because they understand that there is a greater good to be served. They take in many more factors than just who's getting paid what.

They worry about what's happening in other people's lives compared to their own. Perhaps some things that they've been seeking is that now is the time to leave the organization, but when they do it with that sense of personal responsibility and power, they approach what we would think would be an impossible task. I mean, how could anyone plan their job out of existence? How could anyone in their right mind do that? Yet people are capable of making very intelligent decisions that reveal very high levels of power and control over their destiny, but they have to be involved.

Let's take one of the organizations that you have done some consulting with: the US Army. Now, most people's view of the army is that it's very regimented, very structured, very hierarchical. The ideas that you're suggesting—one wouldn't normally associate them with the military organization.

MARGARET: That's right, until you talk to someone who's been in battle, who has been in enormous chaos, or you talk to someone who's very high in the army, who's trying to think about the future needs of the force. Then one of the things that's wonderful about the army—and it is a surprise—is that they are very committed to learning. They know more about their past experience, and they interpret it and they talk to each other. They write about it in internal journals. They're the only example of a real learning organization that we've observed to any degree. Someone said to us, We decided it's better to learn than be dead. I think that's a wonderful imperative. I don't think any of us really enjoys that much more freedom. We all feel really challenged these days to figure out how to make our lives work. The army is very paradoxical. It has very rigid command-and-control structures, but then you look underneath it, and you see examples of leadership that have more love and sense of stewardship in them. You see teams that really know what it is to be a team.

A lot of the things that corporations are trying to create are very superficial training programs about team effectiveness, or leaders who should be compassionate. In the army, there's a very strong tradition, and then there's also this enormous learning that's available to them from anything they've done. They notice that in significant encounters, whether it's Hurricane Andrew or Panama, that when information moved quickly and moved around without rank interfering, people were more effective. They want to notice that, even though it threatens what seems to be a very ingrained system of rank and privilege. If information that's freely distributed makes us more effective, then at least we're really going to look at that now.

MYRON: One of the things that's remarkable in the army is the amount of time and energy they've spent trying to create the conditions where they can actually learn. Most of the ways our relationships are constructed in organizations goes against any possibility of learning. We all know that we're being evaluated by our peers, by our subordinates, and by our superiors. In the army, where you would expect that to be happening all the time, there are instances where they've invested great resources, attention, and commitment to changing those relationships and bringing people together around significant moments to understand what just went on. What did they learn from it? What does it mean for them in the future? The only way they can do that—and this has taken a very long time and it's ongoing—is to make a commitment to an environment that's about surfacing information wherever it comes from. So that the private can say to the general, "Why did you tell us to turn right?" If the general says, "I told you to turn left," they would have the information, and they would be able to talk face to face about it within the context of what we're trying to do.

This contextual linkage is very important. It's what are we trying to do together. What are we learning about what we're trying to do? What have we learned now? You can keep asking that question over and over again. What have we learned now? What does it mean for us now? We don't do that in most of our organizations. We wait a very long time, and then we do an evaluation of each other, rather than what we've done as a whole.

So you are saying that we are bringing much more community into organization, more of a sense of community and a sense of cooperating together toward a common end.

MARGARET: Well, yes, because one of the things that we've kind of misplaced is our understanding that human beings seek to be in relationships with other people. Human beings seek to contribute in their lives. Human beings seek meaning in their lives. Why would we invite those desires into the workplace? All of this work that's being done now—trying to think of organizations as communities—some of it is real sleight of hand. It's just the newest way to manipulate people, to be clear about that. But in some organizations and for many, many people, that desire is to be in relationships with one another in a meaningful context where I feel respected and I have high regard for those around me. Together we're going to create a difference in the world.

MYRON: I'd actually say that that's the dominant impulse of us as individuals. In fact, when we develop organizations where it's not possible to come together that way, we disengage as individuals. Our energy goes elsewhere. That creative energy will find an outlet somewhere else.

We've been talking about community within the organization. That brings up the whole notion of spirit and spirituality. How does that fit within your organizational worldview?

MARGARET: One way of looking at the truly wonderful recognition that people have spirits and people have lives that feel passionate—one way of looking at that is we're finally starting to recognize that you're not this vacant little machine. Work would have been easier if people had been machines. We've tried that for the past several decades. Now we're realizing that unless we know how to engage each other at this deep level of human existence that includes spiritual desires, desire for meaning, desire for relationships, unless we figure out how to do that, we can't create any organization together that can have all the other qualities of life that we need right now.

We're asking organizations to be quick, speedy, fast, flexible, adaptable, resilient, intelligent, conscious, and "learningful." I mean, I pulled these adjectives off of the management literature, and then they sort of wonder, Here we have all these great descriptions of the kind of organizational capacity we want, but we haven't changed our thinking that we can still get there by treating people and the organization as a machine. Well, machines are not adapted. They're not smart. They're not conscious. They're not intelligent. The only category of things that have those capacities are living beings. So this shift that we're trying to make in our work from thinking of organizations as machines to organizations as living systems, is partly being encouraged by lots and lots of leaders and management thinkers who know that they cannot make do anymore or be effective with these great wobbling, rusting mechanistic command-and-control structures that they've created. Now, once you get to looking at life, then you have to get into questions of meaning and spirit and relationships. It's a whole package. So this isn't a superficial shift at all.

MYRON: I also think where does our best work or, to put it into more spiritual terms, where does our best gift to ourselves and to each other come from? There is a way of looking at spirituality that's about being in communion with one another, talking about relationships and connectivity. How does my purpose connect with your purpose? So we create something actually grander than is available to me as an individual. It seems to me that that's also a basic human desire; it is to do more, to be more. That's why I seek you out, Michael, I want to work with you. I want to be with you, whether it's building a community playground in a town, or trying to reshape the economic system of the world. We come together, and we create purpose that isn't available to me, and we create meaning that isn't available to me as an individual. It's only resonant in us as a community. It's that deeper, bigger different power that actually gives us energy and force and commitment and intelligence that goes well beyond me as an individual, which feels spiritual to me. It also feels very accessible to all of us. I mean, we've all had experiences that we call magic. You know, those moments when you've worked informally with a group of people and something's happened where everyone has gone well beyond what they thought they were capable of and done something that they didn't seem to think was available to them before they started.

Do you think that there's a group mind that unfolds in the midst of individuals working together on a common purpose?

MARGARET: Absolutely. It's a very interesting area to think about. Do organizations develop their own personalities? Do they develop their own identities? Well, we've struggled with this for years under the title "organization culture." Now we can call it "organizational mind," but something happens in organizations that is different and not predictable from looking at the sum of the individuals. It's not even saying that it's greater than the sum of the parts. What emerges is different than what anyone would have thought was possible from the individuals. Sometimes it's good and sometimes it's bad, but once it exists, then how do you change it? This has been a struggle in our thinking. It's a struggle in our thinking right now.

The only thing that we're really clear about is that you go back to creating the condition of bringing people together and talking about what we're trying to accomplish and the why of being together. You have these deep conversations about purpose. From that, see if you can create a new organizational mind culture or identity. But these things are so obvious, they're scary to contemplate because you know when you talk about something like organizational mind, you're talking about something that you cannot plan for, something you can't impact simply. We've tried lots and lots of ways of trying to change organizational culture, and very few of them have worked.

It's almost like a myth. You can't really plan a myth. You can't think a myth. It emerges from the depths.

MARGARET: That's right. We think, if you don't like the myth that emerges, you have to go back to some beginning conversation and see if you can start new ones emerging.

MYRON: For me, this is an area that I find exciting and troubling because I think that most of our attention for our communities, our institution, and our organizations, when we go to change them, has been about changing individuals. You know, the way to change my organization is to send everyone in it to a training program that will give them a new mind-set. Then they come back to the organization and we'll all be changed. But if there is really an organizational mind or a community mind, global mind, it may be that it isn't changed by changing the individuals in it. There's good evidence in science that says that there's a dynamic that's put in place that doesn't depend on the individuals. It's affected by it, but it isn't the sum total of individuals. It's just something that emerges from this dynamic interplay of the way people connect and relate with one another.

What about the nature of specialization? We live in an age of specialization. How does that fit within this new organizational idea?

MARGARET: It is very critical, and it's also very problematic because the real work in organization these days is not to develop better specialties, but to figure out to connect people across specialties. So they just don't get this very narrow reduction, this belief that they're right and everyone else isn't important. So most organizations are really trying to figure out how you create these networks and projects. We call them boring things, like cross-functional teams, but it's all about how you use the knowledge of a specialist in a global context. That actually requires a very different kind of training in our thinking. You know, it's not good enough to know your field really well. You do have to be concerned with the whole. Now you can learn that at work by how much access you have to the whole and who you have conversations with and who you're forced to work with, which then changes your perception of your own specialty.

Is something going to happen over the next 10 years, or will it be 20 or 50 years until we see these changes?

MARGARET: I keep changing the estimate. I thought it was 10 to 20 years; now I'm going for seven generations.

MYRON: You experience the change every single moment. We've both worked a fair amount with health care. In the United States, we all know that health care is in some sort of chaos or crisis or opportunity, depending on how you look at it. But that's so in the entire West. Everywhere you go, you find a place that's created, boxes of specialties—all those are beginning to fall away as we go back to some very basic questions, which include: What is health? So we go back to those, and we begin to think differently about what it is we're trying to do by providing health care in our society—for instance, that in those specialties, all the boundaries begin to change and break down. That's happening in every kind of organization that there is.

And that's hopeful.

MARGARET: With changes that are nonlinear, it does proceed by leaps and bounds from strange and unexpected places.

EPILOGUE

Change should be energizing, and chaos is where creativity happens. Beyond the mechanical universe of Newton, we can ask different questions and explore new pathways. Now we can pursue work and meaning, work and wholeness, work and spirit. Wheatley and Kellner-Rogers give us new eyes to see our place in the midst of the organization as a living system and such a view opens whole new vistas of possibility. Since organizations are living systems with all of the naturally creative and self-organizing capacities of other forms of life, we can work within them organically and adapt to change in creative and effective ways. A whole new world of work awaits us.

Recommended Reading

The Art of Resilience: 100 Paths to Wisdom and Strength in an Uncertain World, by Carol Orsborn

Beyond Winning, by Dr. Keshavan Nair

The Coming of the Cosmic Christ, by Matthew Fox

Confessions: The Making of a Post-Denominational Priest, by Matthew Fox

Corporate Renaissance, by Rolf Osterberg

Creation Spirituality, by Matthew Fox

Emerging Women, by Julie Keene and Ione Jenson

The Empowered Manager, by Peter Block

Enough Is Enough: Simple Solutions for Complex People, by Carol Orsborn

Global Mind Change; The Promise of the Last Years of the Twentieth Century, by Willis Harman

The Heart Aroused: Poetry and the Preservation of the Soul in Corporate America, by David Whyte

A Higher Standard of Leadership: Lessons from the Life of Gandhi, by Dr. Keshavan Nair

How Would Confucius Ask for a Raise?: 100 Enlightened Solutions for Tough Business Problems, by Carol Orsborn

Inner Excellence: Spiritual Principles of Life-Driven Business, by Carol Orsborn

An Incomplete Guide to the Future, by Willis Harman

Leadership and the New Science: Learning about Organization from an Orderly Universe, by Margaret Wheatley

Natural Grace: Dialogues on Creation, Darkness, and the Soul in Spirituality and Science, by Matthew Fox and Rupert Sheldrake

Original Blessing, by Matthew Fox

Peak Performers, by Charles Garfield

The Reinvention of Work: A New Vision of Livelihood for Our Time, by Matthew Fox

Second to None: How Our Smartest Companies Put People First, by Charles Garfield

A Simpler Way, by Margaret Wheatley and Myron Kellner-Rogers

Solved by Sunset: The Right-Brain Way to Resolve Whatever's Bothering You in One Day or Less, by Carol Orsborn

Sometimes My Heart Goes Numb: Love and Caregiving in a Time of AIDS, by Charles Garfield

Songs for Coming Home, by David Whyte

True Work: The Sacred Dimension of Earning a Living, by Justine Willis Toms and Michael Toms

When 9 to 5 Isn't Enough, by Marcia Perkins-Reed

Where Many Rivers Meet, by David Whyte

New Dimensions Foundation

Since its inception in 1973, New Dimensions Foundation has presented lecture series, live events, and seminars; published books, sponsored educational tours, and launched a major periodical. Created to address the dramatic cultural shifts and changing human values in our society, New Dimensions has become an international forum for some of the most innovative ideas expressed on the planet. Its principal and best-known activity is New Dimensions Radio, an independent producer of radio dialogues and other programming.

During the past 20 years, many of this century's leading thinkers and social innovators have spoken through New Dimensions. The programming supports a diversity of views from many traditions and cultures. Now is a time for transformative learning and for staying open to all possibilities. We must constantly be willing to review and revise what we are creating. New Dimensions fosters the goals of living a more healthy life of mind, body, and spirit while deepening our connections to self, family, community, environment, and planet.

New Dimensions is a rare entity in the world of media a completely independent, noncommercial radio producer. Primary support comes from listeners. Members of "Friends of New Dimensions" (FOND) are active partners in a community of hope and grounded optimism as we celebrate the human spirit and explore new ideas, provocative insights, and creative solutions across the globe over the airwaves.

You too can play an invaluable part in this positive force for change by becoming a member of (FOND) and supporting the continued production and international distribution of New Dimensions Radio programming.

Become a Member of FOND

As a Member of "Friends of New Dimensions" (FOND), you will receive:

- *The New Dimensions Journal,* a bimonthly magazine containing captivating articles, reviews of books, video and audio tapes, current "New Dimensions" program schedules, selections of audio tapes from our archives, and much more.

- The New Dimensions Annual Tape Catalog and periodic supplements.

- A 15% discount on any product purchased through New Dimensions, including books, New Dimensions tapes, and selected tapes from other producers.

- A quality thank-you gift expressing our deepest appreciation.

- The satisfaction of knowing that you are supporting the broadcast of hopeful visions to people all across the nation and the world.

Contributions are tax deductible to the extent allowed by law.
With Visa, MasterCard, or Discover, please call (800) 935-8273.

A nonprofit tax-exempt educational organization
P.O. Box 569 • Ukiah, CA 95482 • 707-468-5215
Website: www.newdimensions.org • E-mail: ndradio@igc.org

Books, Audios, and More from New Dimensions

(available through Hay House)

Books

Buddhism in the West—The Dalai Lama and other contributors
Money, Money, Money—Marsha Sinetar and other contributors
The Power of Meditation and Prayer—Larry Dossey, M.D., and other contributors
Roots of Healing—Andrew Weil, M.D., and other contributors
The Soul of Business—Charles Garfield and other contributors
The Well of Creativity—Jean Houston and other contributors

Audios

(All of the audios below feature New Dimensions Radio co-founder Michael Toms interviewing some of the foremost thinkers and social innovators of our time.)

The Art of Soul Work—Thomas Moore
Authentic Power—Gary Zukav
Future Medicine—Daniel Goleman
Healing from the Inside Out—Bernie Siegel, M.D.
Healing with Spirit—Caroline Myss, Ph.D.
The Heart of Spiritual Practice—Jack Kornfield
Live Long and Feel Good—Andrew Weil, M.D.
Make Your Dreams Real—Barbara Sher
Medicine, Meaning, and Prayer—Larry Dossey, M.D.
Messages of the Celestine Prophecy—James and Salle Redfield
A New Approach to Medicine—Andrew Weil, M.D.
The New Millennium—Jean Houston
Roots of Healing—Andrew Weil, M.D. and others
Sacred Odyssey—Ram Dass
The Wisdom of Joseph Campbell—Joseph Campbell

Calendar

Wise Words: Perennial Wisdom from the New Dimensions Radio Series

(To order the products above, please call Hay House at 800-654-5126.)

NEW DIMENSIONS
AUDIOCASSETTES

These audiocassettes are the word-for-word recordings of the original radio conversations from which *The Soul of Business* was compiled.

THE NEW STORY IN BUSINESS with **CHARLES GARFIELD**. The "old story" in business and government is one of the rugged individual muscling through a mechanistic world. It's time for a new story, says Charles Garfield, in which we realize our need for interdependence and awareness of one another. Author of the bestselling *Peak Performers: The New Heroes of American Business* (Wm. Morrow 1986), he provides many stories and examples of how the "peak performers" of the future will value collaboration, service, partnership and whatever else it takes to "nourish human beings at the highest levels of their potential." This is the best and future direction for business and, in fact, all human interactions. "It works. It's functional," says Garfield. "It works better than the models we've been using." He is also the author of *Second to None: How Our Smartest Companies Put People First.*

Tape #2345   1 hr. $9.95

DISCOVERING SOUL IN THE WORKPLACE with **DAVID WHYTE**. "The soul would much rather fail at its own life than succeed at someone else's," notes poet David Whyte. "So far, much of (the focus in) corporate America has been about succeeding at other people's lives." Determined to change this situation, Whyte has been working with organizations to help them foster creativity in their employees, for the simple reason that they will not survive without it. It is clearly to the benefit of employers to release oppressive hierarchical models in favor of "another, new kind of loyalty which has to do with a primary, first-hand engagement with life." Drawing upon his deep understanding of the needs of the human soul, Whyte shows us what the next steps will be, and how passion and freedom can be operative concepts in the business world. "We have to take the part of us which does not belong to the work *into* the work," he says. "That's the only way we're going to be able to live now." He is the author of several books including *The Heart Aroused: Poetry and the Preservation of the Soul in Corporate America. Taped at the International Transpersonal Association Conference in Ireland, May, 1994.*

Tape #2479   1 hr. $9.95

WORK, PASSION AND THE LIFE OF THE SPIRIT with **MATTHEW FOX**. Matthew Fox, a former Dominican priest in the process of reinventing his own career, believes work can provide inner satisfaction as well as a paycheck. Silenced by the Vatican and dismissed by the Dominican order for his unconventional teachings, he has turned his passion to reawakening the soul at work. Fox is the author of several books including *Creation Spirituality* and *The Reinvention of Work: A New Vision of Livelihood for Our Times*.

Tape #2482   1 ½ hrs. $10.95

BRINGING SPIRIT TO WORK with **BARRY SCHIEBER.** Step into a realm of possibility where spiritual values breathe new life into our everyday work world. Barry Schieber, formerly a successful investment advisor and now dean of the Nyingma Institute in Berkeley, California, has had decades of training, including five years of solitary retreat, under Tibetan lama Tarthang Tulku, who authored *Mastering Successful Work*. Schieber uncovers some basic questions that will lead us to find meaning and satisfaction in the work we do. More than that, he provides simple, practical exercises—proven methods for dealing with "time handicaps" and the fears that hold us back—to accomplish more than we ever thought possible. Concentrating the mind increases our sensitivity, focus and creativity, and the results are "beyond what we believe we can achieve, once the mind starts to break through the limits. It's quite a freeing experience to realize what we're really capable of."

Tape #2497   1 hr. $9.95

INTEGRITY IN BUSINESS with **CAROL ORSBORN**. Is it necessary to sacrifice health, peace of mind, and spiritual values for success in business? Emphatically not, says Carol Orsborn! Despite the challenges that naturally accompany living with faith and principles, "there was no discrepancy between taking care of myself and my success. In fact, there seemed to be a positive correlation." We hear the story of her rude awakening in a successful business, and the gems of practical wisdom she uncovered in her search for an appropriate, effective approach to the corporate business world. She tells us how to "work with passion and inspiration" and avoid being driven by fear, and shares seven principles for success with integrity. Orsborn is a lecturer, corporate consultant, and the author of *Inner Excellence* and *How Would Confucius Ask for a Raise?*

Tape #2503   1 hr. $9.95

THE SOUL OF BUSINESS with **KESHAVAN NAIR**. What would it take to live a truly heroic, exemplary life, even in the competitive world of business? This longtime student of Mahatma Gandhi shares the lessons he learned from one of the heroes of our century, and how to apply such lessons even in modern life and corporate management. "These principles are not some abstract things that don't have practical application," says Nair. "They will really make you succeed." It is not necessary to have lived up to your ideals, he says, but primarily to take responsibility for being committed to them. That's as much as any hero ever did. True integrity and success are within the reach of anyone. Hear how. Nair is a corporate executive, management consultant and the author of *Beyond Winning* and *A Higher Standard of Leadership: Lessons from the Life of Gandhi.*

Tape #2512 1 hr. $9.95

THE SPIRIT OF SERVICE with **LYNNE TWIST** and **CHARLES GARFIELD**. "There isn't anyone on Earth today who isn't longing to make a difference with their life, who isn't longing for a way to serve and be useful to others. Everyone has a contribution to make." These are the words of Lynne Twist, a founding executive of The Hunger Project. She joins Charles Garfield, founder of the Shanti Project, and together they speak from direct experience of why serving others' true needs is "some of the sublimest pleasure" of human life. Living proof that human nature is founded more firmly on helping others than on competing with them, Twist and Garfield's stories are a powerful inspiration to get on with a life that will fulfill our own spiritual hunger to do some good in the world. Garfield is also the author of the bestselling *Peak Performers, Second to None,* and *Sometimes My Heart Goes Numb: Love and Service in the Time of AIDS.*

Tape #2514 1 hr. $9.95

BUSINESS AND THE FUTURE SOCIETY with **WILLIS HARMAN**. The world is changing—have you noticed? Many of the changes, said the late Harman, may be hidden from view, just as the demise of Soviet communism came as a surprise to many. He saw a number of shifts that would affect us in the near future, and asked us to re-think our assumptions so that we would be ready for them. Harman was president of the Institute of Noetic Sciences, actively engaged in helping realize the future society that we already know how to become. "Just as we as individuals somehow know how to start from a single fertilized cell and become a Michael Toms or a Willis Harman," he said, "this human society already knows how to become a really human society." Listening to this delightful gift of Harman's insight, you will see why. He is the author of *An Incomplete Guide to the Future* and co-author of *Creative Work*.

Tape #2558   1 hr. $9.95

NATURAL CREATIVITY FOR ORGANIZATIONS with **MARGARET WHEATLEY** and **MYRON KELLNER-ROGERS.** The usual approach to work life in an organization does not allow much room for play, risk, or individuality. But principles in the natural world suggest a more creative, effective approach. "Everywhere you look in life," says Wheatley, "what you see is enormous creativity, diversity, and experimentation." She and Kellner-Rogers describe how the same methods nature uses for producing vital, thriving life forms can bring new life to individuals and organizations of all kinds. They tell us how to let go of our need for control, invite innovation—and be ready for surprises! Says Wheatley, "This isn't a superficial shift at all." She is the author of *Leadership and the New Science*. Both are organizational consultants with the Berkana Institute and co-authors of *A Simpler Way: On the New Self-Organizing Paradigm for Organizations*.

Tape #2573   1 hr. $9.95

TO ORDER TAPES
Call toll free: 1-800-935-8273. Each tape is $9.95 unless otherwise noted, plus postage, shipping, and handling.

✦✦✦

We hope you enjoyed
this Hay House/New Dimensions book.
If you would like to receive a free catalog featuring additional
Hay House books and products, or if you would like information
about the Hay Foundation, please contact:

Hay House, Inc.
P.O. Box 5100
Carlsbad, CA 92018-5100

(800) 654-5126
(800) 650-5115 (fax)

Please visit the Hay House Website at: **www.hayhouse.com**
and the New Dimensions Website at: **www.newdimensions.org**

✦✦✦